CRIMINAL
INVESTIGATIONS

ORGANIZED CRIME

CRIMINAL INVESTIGATIONS

CRIMINAL
INVESTIGATIONS

ORGANIZED CRIME

MICHAEL BENSON

CONSULTING EDITOR: **JOHN L. FRENCH,**

CRIME SCENE SUPERVISOR,
BALTIMORE POLICE CRIME LABORATORY

CHELSEA HOUSE
PUBLISHERS
An imprint of Infobase Publishing

CRIMINAL INVESTIGATIONS: Organized Crime

Chelsea House
An imprint of Infobase Publishing
132 West 31st Street
New York NY 10001

Library of Congress Cataloging-in-Publication Data
Benson, Michael.
Organized crime / Michael Benson ; consulting editor, John L. French.
p. cm. — (Criminal investigations)
Includes bibliographical references and index.
ISBN-13: 978-0-7910-9410-5 (alk. paper)
ISBN-10: 0-7910-9410-3 (alk. paper)
1. Organized crime—United States. 2. Crime—United States. I. French, John L. II. Title. III. Series.
HV6446.B44 2008   364.106′0973—dc22
2008016594

Chelsea House books are available at special discounts when purchased in bulk quantities for businesses, associations, institutions, or sales promotions. Please call our Special Sales Department in New York at (212) 967-8800 or (800) 322-8755.

You can find Chelsea House on the World Wide Web at
http://www.chelseahouse.com

Text design by Erika K. Arroyo
Cover design by Ben Peterson

Cover: John Gotti speaks with a lawyer during the first day of deliberations at New York State Supreme Court on Saturday, January 20, 1990.

Printed in the United States of America

Bang EJB 10 9 8 7 6 5 4 3 2 1

This book is printed on acid-free paper.

All links and Web addresses were checked and verified to be correct at the time of publication. Because of the dynamic nature of the Web, some addresses and links may have changed since publication and may no longer be valid.

Contents

Foreword

In 2000 there were 15,000 murders in the United States. During that same year about a half million people were assaulted, 1.1 million cars were stolen, 400,000 robberies took place, and more than 2 million homes and businesses were broken into. All told, in the last year of the twentieth century, there were more than 11 million crimes committed in this country.*

In 2000 the population of the United States was approximately 280 million people. If each of the above crimes happened to a separate person, only 4 percent of the country would have been directly affected. Yet everyone is in some way affected by crime. Taxes pay patrolmen, detectives, and scientists to investigate it, lawyers and judges to prosecute it, and correctional officers to watch over those convicted of committing it. Crimes against businesses cause prices to rise as their owners pass on the cost of theft and security measures installed to prevent future losses. Tourism in cities, and the money it brings in, may rise and fall in part due to stories about crime in their streets. And every time someone is shot, stabbed, beaten, or assaulted, or when someone is jailed for having committed such a crime, not only they suffer but so may their friends, family, and loved ones. Crime affects everyone.

It is the job of the police to investigate crime with the purpose of putting the bad guys in jail and keeping them there, hoping thereby to punish past crimes and discourage new ones. To accomplish this a police officer has to be many things: dedicated, brave, smart, honest, and imaginative. Luck helps, but it's not required. And there's one more virtue that should be associated with law enforcement. A good police officer is patient.

7

Patience is a virtue in crime fighting because police officers and detectives know something that most criminals don't. It's not a secret, but most lawbreakers don't learn it until it is too late. Criminals who make money robbing people, breaking into houses, or stealing cars; who live by dealing drugs or committing murder; who spend their days on the wrong side of the law, or commit any other crimes, must remember this: a criminal has to get away with every crime he or she commits. However, to get criminals off the street and put them behind bars, the police only have to catch a criminal once.

The methods by which police catch criminals are varied. Some are as old as recorded history and others are so new that they have yet to be tested in court. One of the first stories in the Bible is of murder, when Cain killed his brother Abel (Genesis 4:1–16). With few suspects to consider and an omniscient detective, this was an easy crime to solve. However, much later in that same work, a young man named Daniel steps in when a woman is accused of an immoral act by two elders (Daniel 13:1–63). By using the standard police practice of separating the witnesses before questioning them, he is able to arrive at the truth of the matter.

From the time of the Bible to almost present day, police investigations did not progress much further than questioning witnesses and searching the crime scene for obvious clues as to a criminal's identity. It was not until the late 1800s that science began to be employed. In 1879 the French began to use physical measurements and later photography to identify repeat offenders. In the same year a Scottish missionary in Japan used a handprint found on a wall to exonerate a man accused of theft. In 1892 a bloody fingerprint led Argentine police to charge and convict a mother of killing her children, and by 1905 Scotland Yard had convicted several criminals thanks to this new science.

Progress continued. By the 1920s scientists were using blood analysis to determine if recovered stains were from the victim or suspect, and the new field of firearms examination helped link bullets to the guns that fired them.

Nowadays, things are even harder on criminals, when by leaving behind a speck of blood, dropping a sweat-stained hat, or even taking a sip from a can of soda, they can give the police everything they need to identify and arrest them.

In the first decade of the twenty-first century the main tools used by the police include

- questioning witnesses and suspects
- searching the crime scene for physical evidence
- employing informants and undercover agents
- investigating the whereabouts of previous offenders when a crime they've been known to commit has occurred
- using computer databases to match evidence found on one crime scene to that found on others or to previously arrested suspects
- sharing information with other law enforcement agencies via the Internet
- using modern communications to keep the public informed and enlist their aid in ongoing investigations

But just as they have many different tools with which to solve crime, so too do they have many different kinds of crime and criminals to investigate. There is murder, kidnapping, and bank robbery. There are financial crimes committed by con men who gain their victim's trust or computer experts who hack into computers. There are criminals who have formed themselves into gangs and those who are organized into national syndicates. And there are those who would kill as many people as possible, either for the thrill of taking a human life or in the horribly misguided belief that it will advance their cause.

The Criminal Investigations series looks at all of the above and more. Each book in the series takes one type of crime and gives the reader an overview of the history of the crime, the methods and motives behind it, the people who have committed it, and the means by which these people are caught and punished. In this series celebrity crimes will be discussed and exposed. Mysteries that have yet to be solved will be presented. Readers will discover the truth about murderers, serial killers, and bank robbers whose stories have become myths and legends. These books will explain how criminals can separate a person from his hard-earned cash, how they prey on the weak and helpless, what is being done to stop them, and what one can do to help prevent becoming a victim.

John L. French,
Crime Scene Supervisor,
Baltimore Police Crime Laboratory

* Federal Bureau of Investigation. "Uniform Crime Reports, Crime in the United States 2000." Available online. URL: http://www.fbi.gov/ucr/00cius.htm. Accessed January 11, 2008.

Acknowledgments

The author would like to gratefully acknowledge all of the persons who helped in the production of this book. Without their help it would have been impossible. Editor James Chambers, my agent Jake Elwell, private investigator Vincent Parco, court attorney Lisa Grasso, author David Henry Jacobs, Gary Goldstein, Philip Semrau, Nathan Versace, Keith Brenner, Eddie and Cate Behringer, Larry Beck, Scott Frommer, and Carl Soloway.

Introduction

Law enforcement professionals call it knowing your enemy. The more police know about those who break the law, the better chance they have of obtaining justice. Learning about the enemy is called gathering intelligence. Intelligence is particularly important when investigating organized crime, a large group of criminals who are working together. These criminal organizations have established rules and can run with a military-like precision, with a clearly defined chain of command. Organized crime is often more complex than a simple gang, and can entail many gangs that work together for a common criminal cause. Because the organizations are made up of nothing but criminals, there is a high rate of infighting and betrayal within their ranks. Knowledge of the structure of the organization and who works for whom can help police make the correct arrests at the correct time.

That intelligence also includes the history of organized crime, how it has grown in sophistication, how it has evolved, and how it has adapted to police methods to fight it. Organized crime emerged in North America as far back as the early nineteenth century and the days of Jean Lafitte and John A. Murel.

John A. Murel—known as the Napoleon of American Crime—stole the slaves of other men. He was called a "land pirate" and was notorious during the 1830s from Tennessee to Mississippi. Murel's gang included lawyers prepared to take care of any legal difficulties as efficiently as possible. Others were thugs who helped keep the public quiet. The gang stole slaves in great numbers and shipped them to Texas, where they were sold at great profit.

Murel was arrested in 1834 for stealing slaves. According to the Mississippi Local History Network he was later accused of being a member of a secret society called the Mystic Clan, much like the Ku Klux Klan, that routinely murdered black people.[1]

Not all of the pirates of the nineteenth century worked on land. In the years following the War of 1812, Jean Lafitte, who was known as the Gentleman Pirate of New Orleans, took desperate sailors and banded them together into a profitable gang of pirates. He managed to stay out of trouble for years by following one simple rule: He never attacked an American ship.

According to crime historian Joseph Geringer, "Lafitte is known for his piracy in the Gulf of Mexico, and lauded for his heroism in the Battle of New Orleans. Each persona seems to balance the other. He hated being called 'pirate,' for, as he saw it, he was a 'privateer' serving an economic purpose in an economically frugal time in a new country that needed to economize. When he at last sailed away from American shores, he felt betrayed by a country that didn't understand the difference."[2]

Right up until the time of Prohibition, the period of time between 1920 and 1933 when the production, sale, and possession of alcoholic beverages was illegal, America was plagued by loosely organized gangs of bank and train robbers. Modern organized crime emerged primarily in the early twentieth century.

In 1890, a Sicilian organization known as the Mafia first became known following the execution-style murder of New Orleans Police Superintendent David Hennessy. In the decades that followed the Mafia took the concept of organized crime to a whole new level.

Organizing individual criminals into gangs was only the first step. The next came when gangs united and worked together. Such organizations could become hugely powerful. And, because there were so many people working together, crimes committed by such an organization were difficult for police to detect and bust.

The Italian island of Sicily is a tough place with poor soil and a harsh climate. Throughout its history, conquering armies have over-run it. The government in charge was almost always corrupt. Over time the natives, who were mostly poor, began to feel helpless.

Out of this atmosphere was born the Mafia, a secret society, which offered citizens protection from the government in exchange for a fee. They called their society La Cosa Nostra, which means "Our Thing." The term *Mafia*, and sometimes *the mob*, is mostly used by outsiders.[3]

The name *Mafia* has become a somewhat generic term for ethnic organized crime. Today people refer to the Irish Mafia, or the Russian Mafia, but the Mafia discussed here is the one to first arrive in the United States from Italy between 1880 and 1914.

These immigrants were poor and lived in large cities. Jobs were hard to come by. Many of the immigrants—due to their poverty and their experiences in Sicily—thought the federal, state, and local governments of the United States were as corrupt as those in their homeland and weren't giving them a fair shake. Sicily had spent so many years under foreign rule by Greeks, Romans, Byzantines, Normans, French, Spanish, and Austrians that it became an unwritten rule in Sicilian families to leave the government and their police out of private affairs. A small percentage of these immigrants turned to crime and organized themselves along the lines of the Sicilian Mafia. In some cases, crime bosses left Sicily and resumed their rackets in America.

Mafia members live by the code of **omerta**, which means: "Those who call the police are fools or cowards. Those who need police protection are both. If you are attacked, do not give the name of your attacker. Once you recover, you will want to avenge the attack yourself. A wounded man shall say to his assailant: 'If I live, I will kill you. If I die you are forgiven.'"[4]

In the early days of the American Mafia, the top moneymaking racket was extortion. In exchange for money, a man's business would be "protected." If the money wasn't paid, something bad would happen, courtesy of the Mafia. A man's store might burn down in the middle of the night. Or, less subtly, the store would be blown up by a bomb.

Another early Mafia business venture was counterfeiting. In 1909 Ignazio Lupo was tried and convicted of counterfeiting in New York City. Lupo was an underling of crime boss Peter "The Clutch Hand" Morello in what would one day be known as the Genovese family. He was sentenced to 30 years in prison, but he only served 12 years because President Warren G. Harding commuted his sentence.

Prostitution has also been a big Mafia business throughout its existence. The mobsters did not actually run the brothels, however, as this was considered demeaning. Instead, they took a cut of the profits in exchange for protection. Or they came by the brothels weekly to collect the coatroom tips. There were different ways for them to get their percentage.

Bribery was an important feature of mob activities. Cops, judges, and politicians were often paid off to leave the mob alone. These bribes were paid regularly. The officials whose job it was to investigate and arrest the criminals were therefore "on the payroll," employees of those very criminals.

While today legal casinos exist in many parts of the United States, legalized gambling was unknown during the early years of the twentieth century. In those days, the only casinos were illegal and operated by organized crime. These casinos were not huge operations such as the ones today in Las Vegas, Atlantic City, or on various Native American reservations. They were "back room" affairs and functioned behind social clubs, barber shops, and stores. Available were all sorts of card games and slot machines. Another popular form of organized crime gambling was the "numbers" game, which was much like today's legalized lotteries.

During the Great Depression and Prohibition era of the 1920s and '30s, the Mafia grew. The groups of criminals organized into "families," which were sometimes real families, but were called families even if their membership did not follow strict bloodlines. Sometimes the family in question was merely the family of the boss, whose sons were, like princes, expected to take over the family business.

During Prohibition, the Mafia went into **bootlegging**, the production and sale of illegal beer and liquor. Speakeasies—illegal taverns—operated in big cities across the country. Liquor was either made illegally in bathtubs by mobsters or was smuggled into the United States from countries like Canada, where its production was still legal. Not all of these operations were small-time. Beer and liquor continued to be produced in large breweries and distilleries as well.

Not all mobsters got along with one another. Battles took place between rival crime families and within them among their members. Some families competed with other families over "turf," while other families had internal battles over matters of leadership. The Mafia became known as a violent organization, but an organization whose members killed each other more often than outsiders.

Perhaps the most famous example of organized crime violence came on February 14, 1929, when mobsters working for Al Capone machine-gunned to death seven members of the rival Bugs Moran gang in a garage in Chicago, Illinois. This event became known as "The St. Valentine's Day Massacre."[5] Capone, it should be noted, was not associated with the Mafia families in the East. His Midwestern organization at the time was called The Syndicate. In later years, after Capone was gone, it brewed into an organization sometimes referred to as The Outfit.[6]

During World War II the U.S. government first worked side by side with the Mafia as the organized crime group helped provide intelligence regarding the Nazis and fascists who were then in control of Italy and Sicily. Later, the U.S. intelligence services called upon U.S. mobsters who had casinos in Cuba, seeking their aid in ousting communist Fidel Castro from the government of Cuba.

After World War II the Mafia became more aggressive. They sought to take over labor unions. They fixed elections to put their friends in political offices. As illegal drugs became big business in the United States—the new prohibition—the Mafia quickly took over drug-smuggling and sales operations.

At one time there were 26 crime families operating in the United States, which amounted to approximately one per major city. The families were connected via a "Commission," which included the various bosses. In general, the families of New York City and its surroundings were in charge.

For decades, there were many people who denied the Mafia's existence, including Federal Bureau of Investigation (FBI) head J. Edgar Hoover. That is, until 1957, when a meeting of the "Commission"—with representatives from many of the major families throughout the United States—was raided in the small town of Apalachin, New York.

Many people know the popular image of what a typical mobster looks and acts like because mob activities have frequently been portrayed in books, movies, and on television. No criminal element in society has been as glamorized by show business as the American Mafia. *The Godfather* movies and *The Sopranos* TV series are among the most popular depictions, but the process began back in the 1930s when gangster pictures such as *Little Caesar* with Edward G. Robinson helped shape the public image of the classic mobster. One thing Hollywood gets right is the language of the Mafia. In Italian mobs and some others the leader is called the **godfather**. His lieutenants are called ***capos***. Mobsters who are official members of La Cosa Nostra are known as "button men" and "made men." These men have pledged themselves to an organization that started out as an underground government and still considers itself as outside the law.

Unlike TV and the movies, in real life a large percentage of organized crime is not Sicilian or Italian at all. Organized crime comes

Caesar Enrico "Rico" Bandello, played by Edward G. Robinson, points a gun at a shadow of a man he just shot in *Little Caesar*. Robinson's portrayal of Caesar shaped the way the public viewed mobsters. *John Springer Collection/Corbis*

in all ethnicities. This is best evidenced by white-collar crime, such as the fleecing of Enron stockholders by executives from that company, although such outfits lack the element of violence associated with other mobs.

This book will focus on the ways in which law enforcement combats organized crime, but it will be necessary along the way to explain what organized crime is and how it works in order to understand how law enforcement confronts it. Among the techniques law enforcement has used over the years to disrupt organized crime are

- *The Canary.* An informant who is willing to spill his guts about his higher ups in exchange for favorable treatment in the courts.
- *The Mole.* A spy who infiltrates crime organizations and reports back to his superiors what he learns.
- *Legislation.* Congress has passed new laws that make it easier than ever to battle organized crime.
- *Technology.* Electronic surveillance, listening, and viewing devices that make it harder than ever for known mobsters to do anything in secret.
- *The IRS.* The Internal Revenue Service, the government agency that collects taxes. Mobsters don't like to pay taxes, and many a mobster, including Al Capone, has been brought down from a life of luxury to a life in prison because he cheated on his taxes and got caught.

Making Money

Organized crime makes money in many different ways. Sometimes they operate illegal businesses. In other cases they use fear and intimidation to take a cut of businesses operated by others.

For example, if a small-business owner wanted to operate a bar in a neighborhood controlled by the mob, he would have to pay a monthly protection fee to the mob. If he didn't, something bad might happen to the bar, such as a fire or a bombing, or the businessman might be attacked and beaten.

If someone wants to open a pizzeria in such a neighborhood, that's fine, but to avoid trouble with the Mafia, the owner must order the pizza boxes and ingredients from one specified supplier—usually a place owned by a member of the Mafia or someone connected to the mob.

If an entrepreneur wants to open a fancy restaurant or a club, that's fine, but once a week someone from the organization is going to visit and pick up all the coat-check money.

In a similar racket, street hoods charge people parking their cars a fee to watch the car while they're away. If the driver doesn't pay, the car has a flat tire when he gets back. The mob takes this simple "protection" scheme and expands it until they are getting a percentage of many everyday commodities in their community.

It's a form of extortion that seeps its way into the fabric of society. The mob has its finger in many pies. For law enforcement, getting rid of it is more complicated than simply arresting those who are breaking the law. If one part of a crime organization is removed and its members put in jail it is simply replaced with a new part, and the organization continues to function without interruption.

Another organized crime moneymaker is infiltrating and controlling labor unions. The unions were formed to protect laborers from being underpaid and overworked by greedy employers. But, when corrupted by the mob, they can serve to pad the pockets of criminals while leaving the poor working person even poorer and with more work to do.

Criminal organizations also make money by selling illegal products. The mob has been known to sell drugs and counterfeit goods, sponsor prostitution, and provide gambling opportunities in areas where placing a bet is against the law. They also lend money, then charge very high interest rates. This is called **loan-sharking**, and bad things happen to the people who do not pay back their debts on time.

The bootlegging side of the Mafia business began during Prohibition, when alcoholic beverages were illegal. The mob made,

♀ ORGANIZED CRIME AND SPORTS

Mobsters have been involved in sports events in the United States since the early days of Prohibition. Back then the premiere sport for mob activity was boxing. Hoods like Charles "Lucky" Luciano, Al "Scarface" Capone, and Dutch Schultz (born Arthur Flegenheimer) were all involved in promoting boxing cards, taking bets on fights, and fixing fights so the right guys won their bets. By the 1940s "Mr. Big" in the fights was Frankie Carbo, who conducted his boxing business under the false name "Mr. Grey."[1]

Another sport in the grip of organized crime was horse racing. In addition to fixing races—bribing a horse's trainer or jockey usually did the trick—the mob also controlled the news. In those days, race results on the West Coast were sent east via telegraph. By intercepting those signals and delaying their transmission, mobsters could learn the result of a race and place bets on that horse before the news of the winner reached the gambling parlor. In many cases the parlor would be mob-run as well. More sophisticated communication systems—fast long-distance telephone, for example—put these rings out of business.

Today the mob still makes a buck off the sports world. Bookies, who take bets on pro football or other sports, either by phone or through runners (people who run bets and money between gamblers and their bookie), can usually be found to have an organized transported, and sold its own beer and liquor—and made millions of dollars in the process.

The government eventually realized that prohibition was creating a bigger problem than it was preventing. With access to illegal booze, there were just as many people drinking as before, but now criminals were making all the money rather than legitimate businesspeople. The government repealed Prohibition, and alcohol became legal again.

The end of Prohibition put many mobsters out of business. Others adapted and changed with the times. Bootlegging still exists in certain forms. For example, criminals might buy cigarettes in a state or country where the tax on that product is low, then transport the cigarettes to a state where the tax is high and sell the cigarettes

crime connection. Gamblers who run out of money sometimes borrow money from loan sharks and end up owing even more money to organized crime.

Frankie Carbo enters U.S. District Court in December 1959. He was sentenced to two years in prison for his underground boxing operation. *Bettmann/Corbis* at below the market price. Some mobsters moved their operation to the smuggling and sale of drugs. Today drugs such as marijuana, cocaine, and heroin are routinely sold around the world by organized crime families.

Because the mob makes money in so many different ways, it is difficult for law enforcement to completely dismantle an entire organization. Adding to the difficulties is the fact that many criminal organizations also operate legitimate businesses.

Even as famous mobsters are arrested and put in jail, lesser known criminals take their place and the mob continues to take a percentage—known as the **skim**—from many businesses, and the operations work pretty much the same whether they are local, national, or global.

The Mole:
Infiltrating the Mob

You have just been assigned the most dangerous job in law enforcement. You are going to be a "mole." It is more than a nine-to-five job. It is practically a change of identity. You are no longer yourself. You are the character you are playing, like an actor who can never leave the stage. You are a spy, and inside your clothes you wear "a wire," a recording device so that you will leave with evidence that can send the criminals you are investigating "up the river." The job might last for weeks, months, or years—and you can never relax, never let down your guard. You must not get caught. If the criminal organization you are infiltrating discovers the truth, that you are not the person you claim to be, the result will be instant death.

One of the most successful methods used by law enforcement to break up organized crime is the undercover agent. This is a person employed by law enforcement who, after much training, pretends he is a street kid who wants to be a soldier in the mob.

If the undercover agent is accepted into the fold, he learns what he hopes is enough for arrests to be made, and then testifies in court, helping the prosecution convict the arrested mobsters. Being an undercover agent investigating the Mafia is the same as being a spy. The use of undercover agents to gather information or sabotage the efforts of the infiltrated organization is called **espionage**.

Of course, there are millions of places along that route for something to go wrong. In some cases, everything goes well. The mobsters take the bait, the agent is accepted into the family, and hoods are arrested, tried, and convicted. The best example of this is the Donnie Brasco case. One man, as it turned out, put a big hurt on one of the nation's most dangerous crime families, the Bonannos.[1]

Agents who have gotten inside the mob are said to have infiltrated the organization. The goal is for the agent to rise as high as possible within the organization. The higher within the mob the agent gets, the bigger the mobsters he will be able to testify against in court. The agent known by the hoods as Donnie Brasco managed to stay inside the mob for an astounding six years and rose to the level of capo.

Donnie Brasco was actually FBI Special Agent Joseph Pistone. As Brasco he was given the usual beginner's job when it comes to organized crime. He was told to hijack trucks and steal the goods they held. Trucks filled with dresses or furs were best because the items were so easily sold, even though they were hot. From there he gained the trust of his bosses and worked his way up. He eventually got so high up the mobster ladder that he had first-hand knowledge of negotiations between the Bonannos and other crime families in New York and elsewhere. In the long run Brasco, one lone agent, caused grief in several crime families, changing the face of the New York Mafia forever. He disrupted a huge heroin-trafficking operation and supplied evidence that led law enforcement to what became known as the "Pizza Connection" case.

During Brasco's time undercover he was often wired so that his conversations with mobsters were recorded. When he wasn't wired, he wrote down the things he had heard soon after so he would be able to accurately testify about his conversations at a later date. One of the most memorable quotes Brasco dug out was by Benjamin "Lefty Guns" Ruggiero, who explained to Donnie and another undercover agent why it was such a great thing to be in the Mafia. Ruggiero said, "As a wiseguy you can lie, cheat, steal—all legitimately. You can do anything you want and no one can say anything about it. Who wouldn't want to be a wiseguy?"[2]

The FBI knew that, even after all of the evidence was gathered, their case against the Bonanno mobsters would fall apart if something happened to Brasco. To make sure nothing did, the FBI handled it in a way that the mob could understand.

Two special agents, Brian Taylor and Pat Marshall, paid a visit to mob boss Tony Salerno in his home. The agents told the mobster that nothing must happen to Brasco or his family. If it did there would be "massive retaliation."

"You guys have a job to do," Salerno said. "You have my guarantee."

Salerno sent the word out; Pistone (Brasco) and his family were off limits. No violence. And no harm came to Pistone and his family. The agents were impressed by Salerno's gentlemanly behavior.

Much different treatment was in order for the members of the Bonanno family who were duped by Brasco and allowed him access to the information he gathered. Some of those members were killed. Others were kicked out of the family. Add that to the fact that Lefty Guns and his ring of truck hijackers were arrested and put out of business, and the FBI considered the operation a major success.[3]

⚲ JOEY BANANAS

Joseph "Joey Bananas" Bonanno was a hood who made his first million selling illegal booze. During the Roaring Twenties he expanded his network by running numbers games across Brooklyn. During that era Bonanno found himself on the winning side of a vicious mob war, and when the dust settled he was one of the most powerful hoodlums in America, heading his own family.[4]

The hunger for power was Bonanno's undoing. Unlike other godfathers, Bonanno did like to be called "Father" by his mob underlings. He was not in the business just for the money. He saw money as secondary to power. Bonanno knew the other top mobsters saw it the other way around, with power being a byproduct of money. He was planning to bump off the nation's other top mobsters, but his hitman squealed on him. Bonanno appeared before a Mafia Commission and was stripped of his mob power. In 1964 Bonanno was kidnapped in New York City and held captive

(continues)

(continued)

in Buffalo, New York, for 19 months. He was released only after he agreed to retire to Arizona and allow the Commission to pick his successor as the head of the Bonanno family.[5]

Law enforcement did not let up on Bonanno just because he was aging and had been stripped of his power. They called him before a grand jury and asked him to testify about what he knew. Joey refused and was jailed for a time. Unlike most hoods, Joey lived to be very old: 97.[6]

Joseph Bonanno, notorious founder of the Bonanno crime family, leaves the U.S. courthouse in New York after being freed on bail in May 1966. *AP*

The information regarding Brasco and the problems he caused the mob were first made public at U.S. Senate hearings in 1981.[7]

Brasco is just one example. There have been, and there are, many informants who have gotten inside the mob, gained trust, and then reported back to law enforcement so their information could be used to arrest mobsters and interrupt organized crime operations. Many of them, fearing retaliation from the mob, like to keep a low profile, and the public never hears of them. But they are out there, enough of them so that mobsters never know whom they can trust.

The Donnie Brasco case became famous when Pistone wrote a series of bestselling books about his adventures inside the mob, including *Donnie Brasco: My Undercover Life in the Mafia* (1987), *The Way of the Wiseguy* (2004), *Donnie Brasco: Unfinished Business* (2007), and the novel *Donnie Brasco: Deep Cover* (1999), among others.[8] The first book was made into a movie called *Donnie Brasco*, released in 1997.

HOW THE FBI FIGHTS ORGANIZED CRIME

The number one U.S. weapon against organized crime is the FBI, the Federal Bureau of Investigation, the United States' national police. Over the years the bureau has become very good at arresting mobsters and pulling apart crime organizations. This is somewhat ironic because, during the first half of the twentieth century, the federal government did little or nothing to stop organized crime. The longtime director of the FBI, J. Edgar Hoover, claimed that the Mafia did not exist and said that organized crime was a matter for local law enforcement. He was proven wrong, and now, in the twenty-first century, the FBI is the government's number-one tool against the mob.[9]

Since the terrorist attacks of September 11, 2001, the FBI has been concentrating more on homeland security and has had fewer resources with which to combat organized crime. Before 9/11 the FBI had the Italian Mafia on the ropes, routinely indicting and convicting don after don and breaking the power of New York's mob. (A family's boss is known as a "don," a *capofamiglia*, or as made famous by the movies, a "godfather.") The increased need to investigate terrorism has taken a lot of the heat off organized crime and given it the breathing room it needs to grow back.

In a recent press release, the FBI noted that its new streamlined anti-mob strategy has four parts. They are:

- To damage the mob as much as possible with their limited budget.
- Whenever possible, pursue national rather than local criminal organizations.
- Remain flexible enough to pursue regional organized crime groups conducting significant racketeering activity.
- Dismantle or disrupt target organizations.[10]

The FBI is aware of organized crime as a global phenomenon, a problem not just here in the United States but around the world. According to the FBI's official Web site, "The Center for Strategic and International Studies, Global Organized Crime Project, Financial Crimes Task Force estimates global organized crime reaps profits of close to $1 trillion per year. The FBI's fight against organized crime is unlike other criminal programs. Instead of focusing on these crimes as individual events, the FBI's Organized Crime Program targets the entire organization responsible for a variety of criminal activities. The FBI has found that even if key individuals in an organization are removed, the depth and financial strength of the organization often allows the enterprise to continue."[11]

The FBI's stated mission is to eliminate organized crime from the United States. This is done through the use of laws put in place for the express purpose of busting organized crime rings. These laws are called the Racketeer Influenced and Corrupt Organization (RICO) laws, which will be discussed in detail in Chapter 6.

The fight against the mob comes out of The Organized Crime Section at FBI Headquarters, in conjunction with field office executive management. That section is responsible for the overall coordination and support of all organized-crime investigations. According to the FBI Web site, the Organized Crime Section determines priorities, training needs, budgets, and conducts training. In addition to special agents, the FBI Organized Crime Program uses joint task forces with other federal, state, and local law enforcement agencies. It takes a team to fight organized crime.[12]

Informants:
They Call Them Rats

It is September 1963. You are a low-ranking member of organized crime and you can barely read and write, but on this day, you are going to change the world. You are sitting at a long table with two microphones in front of you. Facing you are Senator John L. McClellan and the Senate Permanent Investigations Subcommittee. A national TV and radio audience is tuned in and waiting. Today you are going to do something no one has ever done before. You are an informant, the first ever to spill the secrets of the secret society the world calls the Mafia. Your name is Joseph Valachi, and you are going to give that organization a new name: La Cosa Nostra.

An informant is someone inside a criminal organization, or with knowledge of that organization, who tells police what they know. If this individual is a member of the Mafia, it means that, by talking, he is breaking his solemn oath to never cooperate with the police. But, as it turns out, when a goodfellow is facing hard prison time, solemn oaths don't mean that much anymore. There has been a significant increase in the number of informants in recent years. As La Cosa Nostra grows one generation older and further from its Sicilian roots, young hoods routinely sell out their bosses in exchange for reduced prison sentences. Using informants, law enforcement authorities can successfully break entire organized crime operations.[1]

In most cases it works like this: A low-level member of the crime organization is arrested. A deal is made and the arrested person agrees to inform on his crime bosses in exchange for a short jail term. The boss is then arrested and is urged to inform on his boss. And so on, and so on. If everything goes the way police want it to, they can arrest everyone right up to "the Boss of Bosses," the godfather.

Hoods call informants rats. Prosecutors call them canaries. Ratting out and singing amount to the same thing, it just depends on the point of view. Either way informants are hoods who need a favor, probably because they have recently been arrested and face long jail time. And so they talk to authorities about who and what they know.

JOSEPH VALACHI

One of the best-known canaries, and one that hurt the mob a lot, was Joseph Valachi. He was a mob defector who testified before a Senate committee in 1963. His testimony was so explosive that it was broadcast on TV and radio. It was because of Valachi's public revelations that America got its first clear picture of the Italian version of organized crime, and the public interest in the Mafia has remained high ever since.

Valachi revealed the family structure of Italian mobs, the ceremonies that men must go through, the vows they must take to become "made" members, and the many ways in which the families had earned their riches and built their powerful empires. According to the FBI, Valachi was "the first made member of the Italian gangs to cooperate with law enforcement. Valachi testified that he was a soldier in what he referred to as the 'Genovese Family' named after Vito Genovese who was boss of the family at the time."[2]

Before Valachi sang, he got himself into a jam. It started when he was arrested on narcotics charges, convicted, and sent to a prison in Atlanta, Georgia. Unfortunately for him, it was the same prison that held Vito Genovese, who was still running his illegal operation from inside his prison cell. Valachi earned a reputation as a prison informer (a guy who told guards about other prisoners who were breaking the rules) and life was hard. Fellow inmates tried to kill him three times. In 1962 Valachi thought he was being attacked again. He thought he saw a hitman from the Genovese

Underworld informer Joseph Valachi testifying before the Senate Investigations subcommittee. A U.S. Marshal stands behind him to ensure his safety. *Bettmann/Corbis*

family approaching him, but it was actually another inmate. He went to a construction site in the prison yard, grabbed an iron pipe, and used that pipe to beat the other inmate to death. He claimed he was killing the man to protect himself. Despite the circumstances, Valachi was convicted of murder and sentenced to life in prison.

That is, unless he was willing to talk.

Valachi agreed to cooperate, and from that point on he answered every question the authorities asked.

America learned a lot from Valachi, such as how Carlo Gambino, godfather of the Gambino crime family, had made his early riches. Gambino, Valachi said, earned millions of dollars by selling bootleg food ration stamps during World War II. Because of the war, people were only allowed to purchase so many groceries, depending on the size of their families. In order to buy food people had to use ration stamps. Gambino used theft and bribery to acquire truckloads of food stamps from the federal agency that printed them, then sold them to people who wanted more than their share of goods. Valachi said that he himself was clearing $150,000 a year just as a soldier in the operation. When asked what the families called their organization, Valachi said it was *La Cosa Nostra*, which meant "our thing." They asked him if they used the term *Mafia*. Valachi said, no. That was a term used by outsiders.[3]

Valachi was asked by a member of the Senate committee why there were so many Italian Americans in the rackets.

♀ DON CARLO'S WORDS OF WISDOM

Carlo Gambino, who ran the Gambino crime family in New York City for many years, was born in Sicily in 1902. He was born into an organized crime organization known as The Honored Society, later to become known as the Mafia. He committed his first murders as a teenager and came to America during the 1930s. He made his living during Prohibition as a bootlegger and then as a professional killer for crime boss Lucky Luciano. Gambino rose up the ranks and became a crime boss himself during the 1950s.

When Carlo Gambino was talking to young men whom he wanted to become full-fledged mobsters he would tell them, "You have to be like a lion and a fox. The lion scares away the wolves. The fox recognizes traps. If you are a lion and a fox, nothing will defeat you."[4] Usually those underlings who were listening to Gambino's speech did not know that he stole it from the sixteenth-century philosopher Niccolò Machiavelli.

"I'm not talking about Italians. I'm talking about criminals," was Valachi's reply.[5]

There has been a lot of analysis of Valachi's testimony over the years and it was determined that he testified to more pieces of information than he could have possibly known. It is suspected that he was heavily coached by FBI agents before he gave his testimony, that he testified to items that had been picked up by the FBI's spy microphones, and not things that Valachi had known personally.[6]

The Valachi revelations led to increased funds for battling organized crime, money that U.S. Attorney General Robert Kennedy used to go to war with the mob from 1961 until 1963. It was a war that may have contributed to the assassination of Robert's brother, President John F. Kennedy, in Dallas, Texas, on November 22, 1963.

SAMMY "THE BULL" GRAVANO

Perhaps the second most famous Mafia rat is Sammy "The Bull" Gravano. Salvatore "Sammy" Gravano was born in 1945 in Brooklyn, New York. He was the son of a Palermo dressmaker who entered the United States illegally through Canada in 1920. Sammy was the baby of the family. His father, Gerardo, was 43 when he was born, and Sammy was his only surviving son. An older brother had died of an illness as a child. Sammy knew about the mob from a very early age. Gerardo had to pay protection money to "the *mafiosi*" to keep his Brooklyn dress factory from being burned down.

Sammy was a small kid and a natural born thief. He began to steal not long after he learned to walk. On his way to grammar school at P.S. 186 in the Bensonhurst section of Brooklyn, his routine was to boost (steal) cupcakes for his snack that day from one of the several corner stores that were on his route.

Sammy was never much of a student. He was dyslexic, a learning disability that made it very difficult for him to read. He dropped out of school at 16. He spent a couple of years dividing his time between working in his dad's garment factory and running with a gang of toughs called the Rampers. When Sammy was 19 he was arrested. A cop had tried to break up a street fight he had been involved in. In the heat of the moment Sammy took a swing at the cop and the next thing he knew he was face to face with a judge. The judge said Sammy had two choices, jail or the army. Sammy picked the army.

He reported for duty in South Carolina. The army and Sammy were a good match. He served his two years and received an honorable discharge.

When he got back to Brooklyn he found that his parents had retired and moved to Long Island, but he stayed in the old neighborhood. His sister, Frances, had married a guy named Eddie Garafola, who gave Sammy work now and again in his construction business.

He was 23 years old when he was asked by his old buddy Thomas "Shorty" Spero to join his gang of Mafia wannabes who stole cars and committed armed robberies. Sammy quickly established himself as a fellow unhampered by a conscience. When Shorty needed someone who had double-crossed him "taken care of," meaning killed, he asked Sammy to do the deed and Sammy eagerly accepted the job. Sammy had been told that the double-cross was business oriented but the truth of the matter was that the guy had put moves on Shorty's wife, and Sammy actually whacked the guy because of Shorty's jealous rage. Sammy put two bullets in the victim's brain and learned that he could kill. He didn't have any trouble sleeping at night afterward, either.

Sammy never did grow to be terribly tall. He topped out at five foot five, but he was made out of rock. Despite his size, word of Sammy's effectiveness as a hood made its way up the ranks. He made friends with John Gotti, a brutal yet popular man who was also moving up the organization in the fast lane.

By 1983 Sammy was an acting, although not official, capo in the Gambino crime family. On the streets of New York there were few more respected or feared. But soon thereafter his luck ran out. Sammy was arrested on drug charges and sent to prison.[7]

In 1991 he was pulled out of prison and put in an FBI facility where he was interrogated daily. It was during this time that the FBI first learned the details behind the murder of mobster of Paul Castellano and his driver outside a Manhattan restaurant. Gravano gave detailed information about how John Gotti had taken over the Gambino family. In 1986 the government had tried Gotti on racketeering charges but he'd been acquitted. Gravano now told the FBI that there was a reason for the acquittal. The Gambino family had made it clear to the jury that it was in their best interest to vote "not guilty."[8]

Gravano sang loud and clear. He said that he himself had been involved in 19 murders—all mob hits. He said, "I was the underboss of the Gambino crime family. John Gotti was the boss and I was the underboss. John barked and I bit."[9]

Sammy "The Bull" Gravano testifies at a Senate inquiry into the underworld of boxing in April 1993. *Jeffrey Markowitz/Sygma/Corbis*

In exchange for his singing, Gravano and his family were given new identities and a new home in Tempe, Arizona. He couldn't stay out of trouble, though, and was arrested after his relocation for drug trafficking.[10]

Gravano's new life was provided by the government's Witness Protection Program, which began in 1970. To encourage canaries to sing, the program guaranteed to protect these songbirds for the rest of their lives. To make sure they didn't get whacked, informants were given new identities and were set up in homes far from where they had lived their lives of crime.

FAMILY SECRETS

The use of canaries came in handy for FBI and IRS agents during the spring of 2005, when an informant's statements led to the arrests of 14 mobsters. The indictments involved 18 murders between 1970–86, including the June 1986 hit on Tony "The Ant" Spilo-tro, the Chicago mob's top man in Las Vegas who was buried in a cornfield.[11]

The arrests were the result of a lengthy investigation known as "Operation Family Secrets." The canary in question was Nick Cala-brese, an imprisoned mobster who sang his revealing tune to federal

⚲ BENSONHURST

Bensonhurst is a neighborhood in the southern portion of Brooklyn that has been very important to organized crime over the years. New York's major families—the Gambinos, Luccheses, Colombos, Genoveses, and Bonannos—all ran operations there. Joseph Colombo Sr. lived with his family in a split-level house at 83rd Street and 11th Avenue, near the Dyker Beach Golf Course. Gambino underboss and turncoat Salvatore "Sammy Bull" Gravano lived in a brick row house on 78th Street near 18th Avenue, ran an after-hours social club at the corner of 62nd and 17th, and had his headquarters at Talis Restaurant—called Danzas today by new owners—at 6205 18th Avenue. When a local mobster died, either from natural causes or from getting whacked, people paid their respects at Scarpaci's Funeral Home at 1401 86th Street.[12]

agents. He named names, which allowed investigators to match DNA samples from the suspects with DNA found at crime scenes. Match after match came up in the laboratory, and all of Calabrese's information was proven to be accurate.

Those arrested included James Marcello of Lombard, Illinois, who the FBI said was the head of the Chicago mob, and Joey "The Clown" Lombardo, long known as one of the top leaders of organized crime in the Chicago area.

"The charges announced today are a milestone event in the FBI's battle against organized crime here in Chicago. This is the first investigation that I can recall an indictment that involved so many murders that gets to the heart of what the LCN [La Cosa Nostra] is, and that is a bunch of murderous thugs," said Robert Grant of the Chicago FBI. Arrests were made in Illinois, Arizona, and Florida.[13]

Surveillance:
Wiring Informants, Tapping Phones, and Snapping Pictures

Your name is Willie Boy Johnson and you were a childhood friend of John Gotti's. You're also an amateur boxer. You are half Native American, on your father's side, a fact that has prevented you from becoming a full-fledged "made" man. But it is your ethnicity that directly led you to learn how to fight.

A street fighter long before you ever entered a boxing ring, you retaliated with your fists when kids taunted you, calling you a "half-breed." You were a loan-collector who later, like Sammy the Bull, worked as a government informant.

Because of your abilities with your fists, something you had in common with Gotti, when you were kids you and Johnny Boy were often sent out to "work over" those who were not cooperating with your adult mentors. On one occasion you and Johnny Boy were sent to beat up a man who owned a crooked used car lot that sold stolen cars. And, if it hadn't been for a tiny piece of electronic equipment you two might have killed the guy.

Though you didn't know it, the victim of the beating was under surveillance by the cops. His office had been bugged.

*So, while you and Gotti beat the man within an inch of his
life, police listened in. The electronic device probably saved
the man's life. The cop wearing the headphones heard the
savage beating, called the fire department, and reported a fire
at the lot. The sound of approaching sirens chased you two
away, or else the victim might not have survived the attack.
The victim later refused to tell police who had administered
the thrashing.*[1]

Electronic surveillance is one way to effectively gather evidence
for use against mobsters. For years police have used "bugging"
devices to record sound and video as members of organized crime
discuss their misdeeds.

For years before electronic recording equipment became available, it was common for police to hang out outside Mafia weddings
and take photos of everyone who entered and exited the church. If a
mobster's son was having a birthday party, police would attempt to
get a copy of the guest list. They would stake out the party and copy
down the license plate numbers on the cars dropping off and picking
up kids. They would even glean info from a list of who gave which
present. The higher a hood was in the organization, the bigger his
gift was supposed to be.

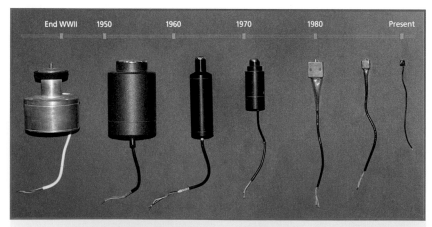

Various bugging devices, arranged chronologically, on display at
the International Spy Museum in Washington in July 2002. Electronic
surveillance is a critical tool for investigating organized crime.
Hyungwon Kong/Reuters/Landov

The first recording devices small enough to be concealed were made during the 1950s, and almost immediately law enforcement began using them to gather anti-mob intelligence. The bugs would be placed in the mobster's phone and home. In the United States it is illegal for police to use electronic surveillance without a court order. For a bug to be legal, a judge must determine that there is reasonable cause to believe evidence of criminal activity will be gathered and grant a warrant for the surveillance. The truth was, though, during the 1950s, the FBI often bugged hoods whether they had a court order or not. They needed the info to further their investigation and, because the bugs were technically illegal, the information that came from them could never be used in a court of law. In memos, agents referred to this information as having come from "secret inside sources." FBI agents became very good at bugging phones and homes very quickly. They would often wear a disguise, such as the overalls of workmen, to gain access to the mobsters' homes.

The resulting tapes were useful to the FBI but often mystifying. The mob spoke in their own language, using vague phrases or code words when discussing crimes. When the infamous canary Joe Valachi agreed to cooperate, one of the first things the FBI did was play for him surveillance tapes of hoods having conversations with one another. Valachi decoded the language so the agents not only knew what was being said, but could understand the language being used in the future as well.[2]

On the Italian island of Sicily, birthplace of the Mafia, police anti-mob operations often involve surveillance. In Sicily the cops use cameras with very long lenses to monitor their subject from great distances. Here's a case where pure surveillance did in a long-time mobster on the run from the law.

Renato Cortese, chief of the special anti-Mafia operations unit at the Palermo police department in Sicily, tracked down mob capo Bernardo Provenzano for eight years. The cop knew the mob boss was worth $600 million, so when he caught up with him during the spring of 2006 on the outskirts of Corleone on Sicily, he was stunned to see how regular he looked. Show business has shaped the public's view of what a mobster is with glamorized portrayals in movies and television, sometimes even shaping the expectations of law enforcement officers as well. When Chief Cortese first encountered Provenzano the mobster was cooking in the kitchen of his farmhouse.[3]

WEARING A WIRE

If it is impossible for law enforcement to place a bug in an organized crime headquarters, or if the criminals have smartened up and only speak freely when they are outdoors, a different type of recording device is sometimes used. A mole may be given a "wire" to wear. This means they spy on the organized crime activity while wearing a recording device, underneath or hidden on their clothes. In some cases the wire transmits to a remote location where law enforcement agents monitor what is being said. Unless the mole is stripped and searched, the criminals have no idea that they are being recorded. Wearing a wire is risky, though. If the recording device is discovered, the mole is likely to meet a quick and violent end.

Cortese later said, "He looked more grandfather than godfather."

The man was dressed simply, in jeans and a thick sweater. He wore glasses. Cortese found it hard to believe that this man was responsible for so much death and anguish, the result of Provenzano's many crimes.

"He couldn't believe that this was happening and that he was being arrested after 43 years in hiding," Cortese continued. "When I went into the farmhouse, it was how I expected him to be hiding. Provenzano probably had a personal fortune of $600 million, but if he had lived a luxury lifestyle, he would have attracted attention."

He was a farmer and he hid in a farmhouse, close to his family, surrounded by sheep and his favorite honey and cheese. Provenzano had surrounded himself with religious pictures, and when arrested he was wearing three crucifixes.

"He had underlined several passages in the Bible which spoke of the fight against good and evil, and he was obviously very religious," said Cortese. "I cannot exclude that during his time on the run, he was not seen by a priest for a blessing or a confession—it's happened in the past. To finally catch this man after eight years was such a fantastic feeling. It was a great triumph and down to good old-fashioned police work. Several times we had come close to arresting him, but he was warned of operations, and we missed him. Once, when we raided a farmhouse he had been using, the embers were still warm in the fireplace. For a man who has millions, it was not the lifestyle maybe you would have expected him to be leading, but we knew that was exactly how he would be hiding. The place was clean and well kept—he had cupboards full of food. There was bread and cheese and lots of pasta that his wife had sent him."

Italian policemen inspect the farmhouse near the Sicilian town of Corleone where Mafia boss Bernardo Provenzano was arrested after a lengthy investigation. *epa/Corbis*

Provenzano was captured though the use of sophisticated surveillance methods. Officers were positioned on nearby hills more than a mile away and used high-tech cameras to zoom in on the farmhouse. The cameras picked up Provenzano as he reached out a window for a parcel of clean laundry that had been sent to him by his wife, Saveria. Phone surveillance had tipped them off to expect the delivery.

"Provenzano's wife made the mistake of arranging for the laundry parcel to be delivered by telephone, and we were listening in," Cortese said. "Although she never mentioned him by name, we followed the parcel as it took three days to cover just under two miles."

The farmhouse was already under surveillance, but so far there had been nothing to see. For days Provenzano never came out. He stayed inside the whole time. When police saw the package arrive at the farmhouse and an arm come through the window to accept it, Cortese had a hunch they were onto something.

"I arranged for thirty officers to come to the farmhouse; they arrived in the back of an unmarked white van. If we had come flying

⚲ LIVING WITH (AND WITHOUT) MOBSTERS

A resident of Corleone, Italy—where mob capo Bernardo Provenzano had made his home—talked to an American reporter after the mobster's arrest about living with—and without—mobsters in their midst.

"In our basic, everyday lives, absolutely nothing changed," said Maria Laura Di Palermo, a 23-year-old Corleone native and university student. "I grew up with an anti-Mafia culture. I was 10 in 1993 when [the boss before Provenzano] Salvatore 'Toto' Riina was captured after 23 years as a fugitive. High school students ran into the streets in joy and rallied behind a banner that read, 'Finally.' I'm 53 now. I remember the 1950s and '60s when there was a killing a day in Corleone. You can image how happy we are about Provenzano's capture. We are very normal people. The name Provenzano only gave an ugly image to our town. If you lived here in town, you'd see we are normal people. The Mafia mix among us honest, kind, open people with a heart."

up the hill in a convoy of cars, he would have been tipped off and long gone. We had to have the element of surprise, and we did. I'll always remember the look in the old man's eyes. I pushed open the door, and he had run toward it and tried to block it, but I managed to get through it. He backed away and looked around, but he knew he was trapped. There was no way out."

Cortese told the mobster, "Provenzano, your time has come. Your time on the run is over. It's time for this to stop and for you to come in."

Provenzano replied, "You are making a mistake."

Cortese doesn't know what exactly he meant by that—whether it was a threat and he was suggesting that he had people in power behind him or he was perhaps suggesting that capturing him might start a Mafia war of succession. "Other than that, he didn't say another word. He just nodded or used gestures when asked questions, and that was it. The look on his face when I arrested him after eight years of nonstop work on this case was something I will never forget."[4]

The Big Bust

There was a time when law enforcement, including the FBI, denied the reality of a national crime syndicate. It was acknowledged that there were some crime families working in some of the nation's big cities, but authorities believed they didn't work in conjunction with one another. People who believed in a coast-to-coast crime conspiracy were quickly dismissed. But that all changed on November 14, 1957, when police raided a large, L-shaped stone farmhouse in the tiny upstate New York town of Apalachin.

The town was just north of the Pennsylvania border. The nearest big town was Binghamton, a couple miles to the west. The stone house sat conspicuously on top of a hill, but the hill was in the middle of nowhere.

The police investigation into that house and the goings on there began in 1956 when a New York State Trooper named Edgar Croswell, along with his partner Vincent Vasisko, found suspicious the activities of a man named Joseph Barbara. What began as good, routine police work quickly escalated into one of the biggest busts in the history of American crime.

Barbara happened to be the owner of the house, as well as the 58 acres to which the house was attached. The truth was, the house was too busy. Even though it appeared to be a normal farm, cars came and went all the time. There was a parking lot out front big enough for 15 cars. None of the other farms in the area needed parking room anywhere near that large. The cars that left that parking lot often seemed to be in a hurry. One time, Trooper Croswell stopped a speeding car after it left the house. Although the driver had fake identification, he was soon identified as mobster Carmine Galante.

The upstate New York home of Joseph Barbara where leaders of Mafia crime families were busted on November 14, 1957. The Apalachin bust confirmed the existence of a nationwide crime network. *Bettmann/Corbis*

Using license plate checks, Croswell and Vasisko determined that other criminals from out of town had visited the stone house. But they let these men go, and did not let on that they knew who they were. They were after the big bust.

There was a good deal of foliage at the bottom of the hill that held the house. Although the house itself was a stone fortress that offered the mobsters security from an enemy wielding a tommy gun, they were vulnerable to spying.

The state troopers, now joined by other law enforcement agencies, set up surveillance points very close to the stone house without being seen, so that the comings and goings at the house could be well documented.

In November of 1957 there were indications that a big meeting was being planned. Barbara's son booked a block of rooms at a nearby motel. One day, cars began to arrive at the house for the meeting. And these weren't just any cars, either. The cops had never seen so many expensive Lincoln Continentals and Cadillacs all in one place.

The feds were notified. As cars pulled in and parked, agents of the U.S. Treasury Department were busy right outside jotting down license plate numbers. As long as the parking lot filled up, law enforcement held back.

The local police forces from neighboring towns had been called in to work as back up. State troopers up and down Route 17 knew what was up and were ready to head toward the scene.

Part of executing a successful raid is timing. If they raided the house too early, those who hadn't arrived yet would get away. The timing had to be designed to maximize the effectiveness of the bust.

Everything went perfectly until one of the observing agents was spotted by one of the hoods. What could have been a neat bust inside the house now turned chaotic in the blink of an eye. Some gangsters ran into the woods.

It was hard for the men to run fast, though, in their dress shoes and tailored suits. Mob boss Joseph Bonanno was among those entering the forest. Another boss, from a different crime family, Vito Genovese, got in his car and tried to make a getaway on wheels, but he was quickly stopped.

A roadblock had been set up on the road that led from the stone house to the main road. Unless they were willing to drive cross-country, no one could reach the main road without going through the roadblock.

Trooper Vasisko told crime writer Jerry Capeci years later that finding the hoodlums who had run into the woods was not very hard.

"All the police cars had to do was patrol the roads," Vasisko said. "The men had to come out of the woods sooner or later. It's

Sergeant Edgar D. Croswell initiated the investigation of Joseph Barbara's house in Apalachin, New York. *Bettmann/Corbis*

hard to blend in with the foliage when you're wearing a silk tie and a white fedora hat."

Altogether, 58 men were apprehended, and although identifying them all turned out to be impossible, it soon became clear that the meeting at the stone house was a national crime syndicate convention.[1]

The nation suddenly learned that the national crime syndicate was a reality. This proved embarrassing to law enforcement officials, especially the director of the FBI, J. Edgar Hoover, who had long maintained that there was no such thing as the Mafia. Some had theorized that Hoover knew the Mafia was a reality but wanted to avoid a war he didn't think he could win. The mob might use its fortunes to bribe special agents and make the bureau look bad.[2]

Now, embarrassed into action, Hoover made a showy attempt to make up for his earlier inactivity. He had rooms and phones of suspected mobsters bugged in cities across the nation. Later, it turned out that the bugs were illegal because no court order from a judge allowing police to listen to a person's private conversations had been obtained. Hoover and his agents listened in on whomever they pleased.

The Apalachin raid was a big blow to the Mafia. People could no longer say that it didn't exist. But, for the most part, the ways

♀ THE ARREST OF VITO GENOVESE

A mobster's worst enemy is often not law enforcement, but rather rival mobsters. Mobsters must live in fear, for their organizations are made up of dangerous and sometimes ambitious men. Mobsters fear violence from members of other organizations as well as from underlings in their own organization who are looking to move up the ladder.

In most cases mobsters are taken out through violence, but not always. When it was learned that mob boss Vito Genovese—who preferred to be called Don Vito—had plans to whack his competitors, Meyer Lansky, Lucky Luciano, and Frank Costello, the three intended victims came up with a nonviolent plan to get rid of Genovese. They set Genovese up for a huge narcotics bust.[3]

The ambitious mobsters used the government's new (1956) Boggs Taylor Narcotics Control Act to arrest the entire gang. The new law allowed judges to sentence drug traffickers to as long as 40 years in prison. Genovese was tried and convicted and ended up dying in prison 10 year later. The 1958 bust of Genovese and 24 of his confederates was a feather in law enforcement's cap, but it was also another example of mobsters behaving like fighting fish in a tank, repeatedly destroying their own.[4]

in which organized crime worked were still pretty much a mystery, and would remain so until six years later when Joseph Valachi sang for a U.S. Senate committee.

A wide variety of law enforcement techniques were used to make the big Apalachin bust. It started with a police officer's keen eye recognizing suspicious behavior. It went on to include the checking of license plate numbers and high-technology surveillance. It concluded with an old law enforcement standby, the roadblock, and the ability of local, state, and federal agencies to work together.

Innovations
and New Law

Al Capone may be the most famous gangster of all time. He was born in Brooklyn at the end of the nineteenth century, had only a sixth-grade education, and was a member of a street gang as a teenager. Another member of that same gang was Lucky Luciano, who also became a famous mobster. During prohibition Capone moved into big time crime as a mob lieutenant and gained great power.[1]

He was rich from his rackets and had bribed many of the right people in Chicago, so he didn't have to worry about politicians or law enforcement getting in his way. When the leader of the Chicago mob, Capone's longtime pal from Brooklyn, Johnny Torrio, was almost killed and decided to retire, Capone took over. It was 1925.

His men were responsible for the St. Valentine's Day Massacre on February 14, 1929, when seven members or associates of the "Bugs" Moran mob were machine-gunned against a garage wall. Capone was in Florida at the time.

The first step in bringing Capone to justice came in 1929 when the feds ordered Capone to testify before a Grand Jury. Capone refused. He was no rat. He had a doctor testify that he had pneumonia and couldn't come into court. A federal operative trailed Capone and found him at the racetrack, and he took plane trips to Pacific islands looking healthy and well.

Capone's archenemy in law enforcement was Eliot Ness, a federal agent with a group of crimebusters nicknamed "the Untouchables." Ness has been dramatized on TV and in the movies, but those portrayals bear little resemblance to the facts. Ness attacked Capone by attacking his business. By busting speakeasies and

Gangster Al Capone, 1928. *Bettmann/Corbis*

disrupting operations whenever he could, Ness hurt Capone finan-
cially. With less money, Capone could bribe fewer public officials
and became easier to investigate.[2]

On March 27, as Capone left the courtroom, he was arrested by
agents for contempt of court. He was charged with lying (a crime

called perjury) when he said he was sick, an offense for which the penalty could be one year in jail and a $1,000 fine. He posted $5,000 bond and was released. He was arrested again two months later, this time for carrying concealed deadly weapons. Al was packing heat, a gun. In less than a day he was tried and convicted and sentenced to a year in jail. He served nine months in Eastern Penitentiary in Philadelphia, Pennsylvania.

He was free for less than a year when he was finally tried and convicted on the contempt charges. Found guilty, he did six months in the Cooke County Jail. But that was nickel-and-dime stuff. The thing that finally sank Capone was the fact that he did not pay taxes. This is the first and best example of putting a mobster behind bars by following his money.

Agents of the U.S. Treasury grilled all of Capone's accountants. They inventoried all of Capone's belongings. They developed evidence that Capone was making millions of dollars through his rackets and was paying tax on none of it. He was finally arrested on those charges, along with several other mobsters who had been caught up in the same investigation.

On June 16, 1931, Al Capone pleaded guilty to tax evasion. After the hearing he told reporters he'd cut a deal with prosecutors for a light sentence. When the judge heard this he told Capone that he was bound by no deal made by a prosecutor. In other words, the judge could sentence Capone to as long a prison term as he wanted, as long as the law allowed. This took Capone by surprise and he changed his plea to not guilty. After a failed attempt to fix the jury, Capone was convicted that fall and sentenced to 11 years in a federal prison. He was fined $50,000 and charged $7,692 for court costs, in addition to $215,000 plus interest due on back taxes.

Capone served his sentence in Alcatraz, the notorious prison on an island in the middle of San Francisco Bay. He served seven years but, by the end of 1939 when he got out, he was a sick man. He had syphilis and had grown mentally and physically weak with his illness and he was never again capable of being a mob boss. By 1947, the year he died of a stroke, his brain had rotted away to the point where, according to the FBI, he had the mentality of a 12 year old.

Today, the benefactors and perpetrators of organized crime operations are smarter about money matters than they used to be, and they have smarter accountants. It has become increasingly difficult to prosecute mobsters on tax charges because they are so much

Eliot Ness, Director of Cleveland Federal Alcohol Tax Bureau, October, 1936. Ness was a primary figure in the investigation of Al Capone.
Bettmann/Corbis

better at disguising the amount of money they make and spend, where it comes from and where it goes.[3]

One of the ways the government has combated organized crime through the last half century is by passing laws making it easier to arrest and convict mobsters. The most effective of these laws have been the so-called **RICO Laws**. RICO stands for the Racketeer Influenced and Corrupt Organizations Act. It is suspected that the name was chosen because a character named Rico was the big cheese in an old-time gangster movie called *Little Caesar*.

Congress passed the set of laws in the fall of 1970. It allowed law enforcement to arrest mobsters who were part of a conspiracy to commit a crime. Anyone who was part of an organization that was committing a crime and helped that organization commit the crime was guilty of committing the crime, whether or not they actually pulled the trigger or robbed the bank. The crime was called racketeering, which meant conspiring with others to profit from an illegal business of some sort.

There are actually 35 different crimes for which one can be found guilty using the laws supplied by the RICO Act. These include

- bribery
- counterfeiting
- theft
- embezzlement
- fraud
- dealing in obscene matter
- obstruction of justice
- slavery
- racketeering
- gambling
- money laundering
- commission of murder-for-hire
- gambling
- murder
- kidnapping
- arson
- robbery
- extortion
- dealing in a controlled substance

Racketeering laws became a new weapon against mobsters. Those convicted could get 20 years in a federal penitentiary, be fined $25,000, and be forced to give back all of the money earned through illegal business. Now, people who had lost money through a mob scheme could sue the mobster to get their money back in

♀ AUTHOR OF THE RICO ACT

The Racketeer Influenced and Corrupt Organizations Act was written by a law professor named G. Robert Blakey, who came up with ideas to battle the mob via his think tank, the Notre Dame Institute on Organized Crime. Blakey realized that because organized crime was so complex, there was a great social distance between the bosses who ordered crimes to be committed and the soldiers who actually committed them. Law enforcement needed a law that made it illegal to operate a criminal organization. Such a law would mean law enforcement would no longer have to prove that a crime boss directly ordered a crime to be committed. Now they would just have to prove that the boss ran the organization, and the organization had committed the crime. Blakey originally intended the law to make it harder for criminals to hide their illegal activities by infiltrating the legitimate business world. Once the law was written, however, he realized it could be used to curtail all criminal enterprises.[4]

Blakey is also well known for his two-and-a-half-year investigation into the assassination of President John F. Kennedy, during which he concluded that key mob figures had the ways and means to have assassinated JFK.[5]

triplicate. Few did. Common sense told most people that suing a mobster wasn't the smartest—or safest—idea.

On November 21, 1980, Frank "Funzi" Tieri became the first mobster convicted using the RICO laws.[6] The new law allowed criminals to be prosecuted for a "pattern of racketeering activity." Tieri was charged with being the head of a criminal organization that had committed murder, extortion, illegal gambling, fraud, and narcotics trafficking. Tieri was a sick and old man by the time he was convicted and sentenced to 10 years in prison. He died in a New York hospital two months after his 1981 sentencing.[7]

Other Mobs

During the spring of 2006 the FBI and New York Police Department teamed up to bust a pair of mobsters who had committed two murders back in 1992. But these were not members of the Italian mob. They were Russians and "made men" in the Russian mob. The cops didn't care. A hood is a hood is a hood as far as they were concerned.

The victims were a suspected informant and a pool hustler killed in a robbery gone bad. The cases lay unsolved for years until new evidence was gathered. Concerned citizens spoke up about what they saw, and frightened hoods spoke up about what they knew. According to cops, the murders were the idea of young mobster wannabe Marat Krivoi, who ran a tough crew of thugs with an eye toward impressing his father-in-law, Russian mob don Boris Nayfeld.

Following the arrests, Brooklyn District Attorney Charles J. Hynes said, "This should remind all criminals that they can never be sure that the long arm of the law won't grab them when they least expect it."[1]

Under arrest were Krivoi, his buddy Vitaly Ivanitsky who, along with another unnamed man, lured the suspected informer, 21-year-old Boris Roitman, to a deserted spot in outer New York City where they blasted him twice with a shotgun. After the first blast, Krivoi is said to have ordered, "Shoot him again. Make sure he's dead."

In the second killing, Krivoi and Ivanitsky ambushed a local pool hustler, Thien Diep, 24, as he got into his car outside a pool hall in Coney Island. As Ivanitsky drove, Krivoi held a gun to the man's head and demanded money. When Diep refused to take the men to his home, Krivoi shot him.

The story proves two points. The first is that law enforcement is always working to apprehend and punish the guilty.[2] The second is that although America and the rest of the world may be fascinated with the Italian Mafia because of the powerful public figures, colorful characters, and funny nicknames it has produced, organized crime comes in all nationalities, races, and ethnicities—and it operates on a global scale.

JAPANESE MOB: YAKUZA

Yakuza is a Japanese organized-crime group. The word *Yakuza* means "eight-nine-three," for a total of 20. This is symbolic of being a loser in society because it refers to a card game called *Oichu-Kabu*. In this game, similar to Blackjack, the perfect number is 19 rather than 21; therefore, 20 means you lose.

Yakuza dates back to the early seventeenth century, evolving from a group known as *Kabuzi-mono* (crazy ones)—criminals known for their slang speech, long swords, and distinctive clothing and hairstyles. The kabuzi-mono were bands of robbers who attacked villages and small cities, sometimes murdering for fun as they looted and pillaged. Today's Yakuza prefer to trace their ancestry back to a mythical group known as *machi-yakko* (city servants), a Robin Hood-like band who were the enemies of the kabuzi-mono, and have been the heroes of many fictional stories. The Yakuza, under that name, first appeared in the mid-seventeenth century. They were gamblers and street vendors who were loyal to one another in times of conflict. Given a choice between loyalty to one's Yakuza comrades or one's own family, Yakuza would stand by Yakuza.

Today's Yakuza are almost all, like their predecessors, poor misfits of society who have turned to crime because they lack more honorable opportunities. For these people, Yakuza becomes their family, and that is how Yakuza members organize themselves. The father figure is referred to as *oyabun* and the children called *kobun*. Since the mid-1800s, the initiation ceremony into Yakuza involves the ceremonial drinking of sake, a Japanese alcoholic beverage made from rice.

Today's Yakuza are divided into three groups.

Tekiya. Street vendors, who operate in Japan's markets and fairs, evolved from peddlers of questionable medicines, much like snake-oil merchants of the American Old West. The tekiya are known for their shoddy merchandise and con-man techniques. It is common for tekiya to pretend to be drunk so that customers buy products, thinking they are taking advantage. In reality, it is the other way around. Today's tekiya participate in protection rackets and the harboring of criminals.

Bakuto. Gamblers, the bakuto gained power when they were hired by government construction and irrigation firms to gamble with the firm's employees in an effort to get back a portion of the wages paid to the laborers. (A similar scheme is used in Atlantic City and Las Vegas, where show business personalities and boxers are paid by the casinos partially in chips in an attempt to get a portion of their payroll back in the casinos.)

A former Yakuza member displays his tattoos and two prosthetic fingers disguised by gold rings. *TWPhoto/Corbis*

The bakuto originated the ceremonial cutting off of someone's fingers associated with Yakuza honor. This is called *yubitsume*. The top joint of the little finger is ceremoniously chopped off as an apology for an infraction, or as a punishment. This amputation signifies the weakening of the hand, which means the member of the bakuto can no longer hold his sword so tightly. If an individual must undergo yubitsume more than once, either the top joint of another finger is chopped off, or the next joint of the little finger.

Bakuto are sometimes ceremoniously tattooed with a black ring around the arm as apology or punishment. The tattooing process for a solid black ring is painful and can take up to 100 hours.

Gurentai. Hoodlums, this last group emerged as part of Yakuza after World War II.

In the second half of the nineteenth century, Japan went through a modernization period, and the Yakuza modernized as well. They recruited construction workers and gained control of the rickshaw business. The police were cracking down on bakuto gangs so the gamblers became more secret in their activities. The tekiya continued to operate in the open and expanded their activities during this time period.

Yakuza went into politics, supporting certain politicians and campaigning against others. The Yakuza became an important part of the nineteenth-century Japanese movement, which used a secret military to force Japan into adopting democracy.

A reign of terror, using Yakuza as its henchmen, continued until the 1930s. During the movement, two prime ministers and two finance ministers were assassinated. There were several attempts to overthrow the Japanese government. After the Japanese attack on Pearl Harbor, however, Japanese priorities changed. Many members of Yakuza joined the army.

After World War II the Americans occupying Japan tried to wipe out Yakuza, but their attempts were unsuccessful. The Americans had rationed food, and Yakuza went into the black market, selling illegal food. Yakuza became wealthy and powerful during this period, and Japan's civil police, who were not allowed to carry weapons, were defenseless against them. The leaders of this black market were the gurentai. In 1950 the Americans stopped their battle against the Yakuza. The Yakuza became increasingly violent during this decade. They stopped carrying swords and started carrying guns. They began to look like American gangsters, with dark suits and ties, crew cuts, and sunglasses. By 1963 it was believed that Yakuza had 184,000 members. Various Yakuza gangs went to war against one another over turf. During that time a man named Yoshio Kodama managed to convince the leaders of the various Yakuza factions that in-fighting helped no one, and that there were many benefits to operating as a single coalition. His plan worked. Kodama has been referred to as "the Japanese underworld's visionary godfather."

On March 1, 1992, the Japanese government passed the Act for Prevention of Unlawful Activities by Boryokudan (Yakuza and other criminal gangs). Legally, the definition of *boryokudan* is any group with a certain percentage or higher of members who have a criminal record. Although it is not illegal to be a member of these groups, the act prohibits these groups from partaking in forms of extortion that are not specifically banned by previously existing laws. The act was a blow against the Yakuza protection rackets.

In order to avoid being classified as a boryokudan, the Yakuza has once again moved underground, using legitimate organizations as fronts. As the millenium began, almost 80 gangs had registered as businesses or religious organizations. There have been several public protests by Yakuza members claiming that they are not criminals as they are publicly perceived, but these efforts were overshadowed by the death on December 20, 1997, of filmmaker Itami Juzo, who made an anti-Yakuza film called *Minbo no Anna* ("Gentle Art of Japanese Extortion"). Though the filmmaker's death was officially ruled a suicide, it is widely believed that he was murdered by the Yakuza.

Yakuza remains very powerful and rumors persist that they continue to have an impact on Japanese elections through both legal and illegal means. There are also rumors that, since it is more difficult to operate inside Japan, more Yakuza members will come over to the United States to set up business, a possibility for which the FBI is already gearing up.[3]

CHINESE MOB: THE TRIADS

The Triads are popularly known as the Chinese Mafia. This group has their hands in drug trafficking, prostitution, gambling, robberies, murders, and a gruesome series of torture methods for those who cross their path.

The Triads were secret criminal societies organized in the 1800s to battle the rule of the Chinese Dynasty. Like the Sicilian Mafia, they were formed in response to a corrupt government. They continue to this day to flourish in Hong Kong, Malaysia, Singapore, Thailand (then called Siam), Burma, and Taiwan. Triads operate in Great Britain and Australia, having migrated from Hong Kong, and also in the United States.

According to Hong Kong police, the Triads are far more loosely structured than the Mafia. The bosses of Triad groups are highly respected and feared, but they don't necessarily determine their soldiers' every move, and soldiers do not necessarily share their ill-gained profits with their bosses.[4]

Law enforcement agencies around the world attack the Triads using the same methods used to battle other forms of organized crime. When low-ranking members are arrested, they are encouraged to gather evidence and testify against their bosses, and are often offered deals in exchange for this testimony.

Moles are trained and placed inside Triad groups so that police can anticipate upcoming crimes and take apart criminal operations. One of the more successful busts using this method came in 2002 in Hong Kong in which police spies placed inside a Triad group facilitated the arrest of 60 Triad members and 90 drug traffickers with Triad ties.[5]

One of the Triad's top businesses is the smuggling of illegal aliens. Triad members who engage in this activity are so-called snakeheads. For $15,000 commission, a Chinese-based snakehead will smuggle an illegal alien into the United States. The alien is always promised a job when they arrive. Once the commission is paid, the alien learns that the conditions of the transfer to the United States involve no sanitation and cruel overcrowding during transportation. Those who survive the trip quickly learn that no job is waiting. Many of these illegal aliens, in order to survive, become Triad members in cities like Chicago, so the system feeds itself.

Another Triad business is the selling of drugs, in particular "ice," the smokable form of methamphetamine. There is evidence that the Chinese gangsters are working in conjunction with non-Asian gangs in the United States, such as street gangs like the Bloods and the Crips.[6]

⚲ ASIAN/AFRICAN CRIMINAL ENTERPRISE UNIT

It might seem that Asian mobsters are another country's problem, but this is not the case. These organizations are global and the FBI has a hand in controlling them, and, as best as possible, keeping their members and activities out of the United States. Asian mob investigations are based at FBI headquarters and are run by the Asian/African Criminal Enterprise Unit of the bureau's Organized Crime Section.

According to the FBI, "This is done through the use of sustained coordinated investigations utilizing innovative and sophisticated investigative techniques. FBI Special Agents target known criminal enterprises, utilizing the RICO laws to dismantle and disrupt these criminal enterprises in accordance with the FBI's Organized Crime Program strategic plan. . . . This unit also works to enhance the relationship between the FBI and other federal agencies as well as agencies of other local, state, and foreign governments, through national and international working groups and initiatives, regional and national conferences, training programs, and police exchange programs. This unit also works to enhance and coordinate the sharing of criminal intelligence between the FBI and the United States intelligence community as it relates to Asian/African Criminal Enterprise investigations."[7]

CYCLE GANGS

Motorcycle gangs—such as the Banditos, Outlaws, Hessians, and Devil's Disciples—are organizations that have been known to participate in organized crime. Among the crimes members of these groups have been convicted of are drug trafficking, murder, assault, prostitution, and extortion. The most famous motorcycle gang is the Hells Angels (there is no apostrophe in the name of the club). The Hells Angels Motorcycle Club was formed in 1948 in San Bernardino, California. Since then, chapters of the club have opened across the United States and around the world. While publicly presenting itself as a club of motorcycle enthusiasts who enjoy riding Harley-Davidson motorcycles, frequent arrests have shown that

Ralph "Sonny" Barger, founder of the Hells Angels Motorcycle Club, September 2002. *Carmen Jaspersen/dpa/Corbis*

the club is—at least in part—a front for organized-crime activities, including the illegal distribution of firearms and the sale of drugs. Defenders of the organization say that 99 percent of the members are law abiding.

The most famous member of the group is former Oakland-branch leader Sonny Barger, who arranged for the Hells Angels to supply security at the ill-fated 1969 Altamont concert featuring the Rolling Stones. The Hells Angels accepted $500 worth of beer to police the concert, but one member of the club stabbed a spectator to death in front of the stage after the victim pulled a gun.

Membership is achieved through invitation only. "We don't recruit members, we recognize 'em," is the motto. New members must endure a hazing-type initiation process. Members get to wear denim jackets with the Hells Angels logo (the groups "colors") sewn onto the back.[8]

Famous Rubouts

It's December 1985 and there are only a few more shopping days left before Christmas. You are an innocent pedestrian walking along East 46th Street in New York City, carrying shopping bags, and heading for the subway home. Shopping took longer than you had planned. It's already dinnertime. Rush hour traffic is already starting to let up. Just as you are walking past an awning with the word "SPARKS" written on it, a limousine pulls up to the curb and two men get out. Then, suddenly, there is chaos. Men on the sidewalk pull out guns. Shots are fired. Both of the men who got out of the car fall to the pavement and are still. There is the sound of running feet, screams, and squealing tires at the end of the block.

You have just been a witness to a major organized-crime "rubout," gangsters killing other gangsters. What do you do? You got a pretty good look at the gunmen. You could probably pick them out of a police lineup. Do you call 911 and tell the police what you saw? No way. You walk faster, your heart racing, and get away from there as fast as you can. Anyone with any street smarts knows that squealing on members of organized crime can be a big mistake.

As long as no one innocent gets hurt, law enforcement doesn't mind that much when differing factions of organized crime go to war against one another. Mobsters killing other mobsters is one brutal but efficient way of getting criminals off the streets. That isn't to say that police will not investigate mob rubouts. They will, and if they gather enough evidence against a suspect they will be arrested and tried in a court of law. But if there is no good evidence and the crime goes unsolved, no one in law enforcement is heartbroken.

There are a number of reasons why some organized crime figures kill other organized crime figures, including the following:

- disputes over turf or territory
- a perceived loss of honor
- revenge
- because one organized crime leader is power-hungry and greedy, and perceives one of his competitors as weak

Sometimes hoods are hit not by a competing family but by hit men within their own family, as punishment for disobeying orders. The bottom line is that mobsters often kill each other, thus bringing criminals to justice without law enforcement involvement.

Rubouts are often committed in public for a couple of reasons. For one, it is usually easier to get to a mob figure in public. His home is often built like a fortress with tight security. For another, killing a man in public in front of many witnesses sends a wave of fear through the community. The witnesses are almost always too frightened to tell police what they saw and an unspoken message is sent out loud and clear: Bad things happen to those who tick off mobsters.

This chapter details some of the famous mob rubouts over the years, or "whackings," as mobsters call them.

MOBSTER GONE WILD

On October 25, 1957, mobster Albert Anastasia was whacked in the barbershop of the Park Sheraton Hotel at 56th Street and Seventh Avenue in Manhattan. He was getting a haircut at the time. Anastasia had been making enemies wherever he went. He wanted a larger piece of other mobster's pies, and he had earned the nickname the "Mad Hatter" for his primitive and unpredictable ways. When he was around, people tended to get hurt, and other mobsters had decided it was time for it to stop. Whacking Anastasia was the idea of Vito Genovese, working with Carlo Gambino, an Anastasia underling who figured to take over the organization after Albert's death.

Anastasia didn't have a chance. Even his bodyguard was in on the deal. The bodyguard parked Anastasia's car in the garage beneath the hotel. He then went for a walk rather than sticking close to the man he was hired to protect.

With Anastasia in the barber chair, two men wearing scarves over their faces rushed in, pushed the barber to safety, and then opened fire on the guy in the chair. Anastasia leaped up and dove in the direction of the mirror in front of him, but it was too late.[1]

"LEGS" DIAMOND

Jack "Legs" Diamond was one of the nation's top hoodlums from 1919 until his death in December 1931. When he was finally killed it came as no surprise. The Irish hoodlum had survived many attempts on his life before that one. It has been estimated that he'd been hit by 17 bullets in previous incidents. It was presumed that the hit attempts were being made by Diamond's primary rival, Dutch Schultz. Once, Legs had been standing in front of his hotel catching some air when a drive-by shooting occurred, with a tommy gun. Legs was hit three times and two others were killed.

Another time rival gangsters came upon Legs when he was in a restaurant having a meal with his mistress. He was shot five times and wounded badly enough that he had to spend several weeks in the hospital.

For the fatal hit, Legs was asleep in an Albany, New York, hideout after a night of drinking. Hoods broke into his room, pulled him out of bed and propped him against the wall before shooting him dead.[2] Three bullets were fired into Diamond's brain and it was over. The killers were never caught, but it was assumed they were Shultz's boys. When police questioned Legs' wife about his death, her first comment was, "I didn't do it."[3]

CIGAR SNUFFED

Brooklyn may lead the world in most mob hits per square foot. One of the most famous hits to take place in the so-called Borough of Churches was that of Carmine Galante on July 12, 1979.[4]

Galante was a capo in the Bonanno family and was nicknamed "Cigar" because he always had one in his mouth.

Galante was murdered as he lunched at Joe and Mary Italian-American Restaurant in the Bushwick section of Brooklyn. He ate outside, in a little garden in the back. The killers shot him in the face and chest with a shotgun and then escaped in a stolen car. Also killed in the attack was the restaurant owner, who was Galante's cousin.

The hit became famous when a photo in the morning newspaper showed that even in death, Galante still had a cigar clenched between his teeth. It has long been assumed that Galante's murder was a power play by rival mobsters.[5]

"MOMO" NO MORE

Sam "Momo" Giancana, who ruled over Chicago, was cooking his own dinner when his life came to a sudden halt on June 19, 1975. Giancana was considered ruthless even in a world of ruthless men. His life had been spent removing obstacles that were in his way, even if (maybe especially if) those obstacles were human beings.

In the early 1960s Giancana helped the Central Intelligence Agency (CIA), with money and personnel, in covert operations within Cuba to rid that country of its communist leader, Fidel Castro. For a time, Giancana and President John F. Kennedy shared a mistress, a woman named Judith Exner. She later claimed to have passed messages between the two.[6] Giancana wasn't known for his ability to keep a secret. When the CIA/Mafia teams were planning to assassinate Castro in 1960, J. Edgar Hoover got wind of the plan because Giancana "told several friends."

According to Giancana's half-brother, Charles (Chuck), and his nephew, Sam, in their book *Double Cross* (1993), President Kennedy was murdered by a team of Chicago hitmen sent to Dallas by Giancana. The fatal shot, they claim, was fired by Giancana lieutenant Richard Cain, from the Texas School Book Depository's sixth floor. Cain himself was murdered in 1973, "gangland style."[7] The book also claims that Giancana ordered the murder of his mistress Marilyn Monroe, who was supposedly killed by Giancana henchmen with a poison suppository.

Giancana had been talking to a Senate intelligence committee when he died on June 19, 1975, at age 67. Despite what was

Gangster Sam "Momo" Giancana handcuffed to a chair in a police station. He was assassinated in his home on June 19, 1975. *Bettmann/ Corbis*

supposed to be constant police protection, Giancana's assassin had no trouble getting into Giancana's home. The Chicago boss was shot with a .22 pistol once in the back of his head and six times around his mouth—a Mafia symbol for "talks too much." He was shot in the basement of his Oak Park home. The murder weapon was later found on the bank of the Des Plaines River.[8]

FLOATER

Johnny Roselli was killed around August 7, 1976, off the coast of Florida. Roselli was a powerful asset to both organized crime and the CIA's efforts to rid Cuba of Fidel Castro, who had declared himself an enemy of the United States. The CIA had hired Roselli and other organized crime figures to orchestrate the assassination of Castro. The criminals took the CIA's money, but never came close to killing the Cuban leader.[9]

Roselli was a high-ranking member of the Chicago organized crime organization sometimes called "The Outfit." He had been a key reason that The Outfit had gained control of the Las Vegas strip and much of Hollywood.[10]

Roselli started as a street hood in Chicago working for Al Capone. Roselli was one of organized crime's most powerful figures until the murder of The Outfit's boss, Sam Giancana, which left Roselli without a power base and vulnerable to the law. He decided to cooperate with law enforcement in hopes of getting the best deal possible. Only days after agreeing to testify to the Senate and speaking to columnist Jack Anderson, Roselli was garroted, stabbed, and dismembered, left to float in an oil drum off the coast of Florida in August 1976. His date of death is officially listed as August 7, 1976.[11]

FINAL MEAL

The whacking of Joe "The Boss" Masseria changed mob history. Masseria was murdered on April 15, 1931, in the Coney Island section of Brooklyn. His violent death helped to put into place the mob leadership that would remain for most of the rest of the century.

Masseria had been in a war with Sal Maranzano. Both men wanted to be boss of all the crime families, not just the one he ran. Sal was a visionary of sorts. He saw a world in which the families worked together rather than warring amongst themselves, thus increasing La Cosa Nostra's power. Sal saw the "big picture." Masseria couldn't have cared less about Maranzano's vision. Masseria had a vision of his own, one in which New York City was all his. The war went on for two years and resulted in lots of guys getting bumped off on both sides.

Bugsy Siegel, Meyer Lansky, and Lucky Luciano had a clandestine meeting with Sal in the Bronx Zoo. There, while feeding peanuts to the elephants, they came up with a way to end the war: Joe had to go. So Luciano asked Joe to join him for dinner at Scarpato's in Coney Island on April 15, 1931. The men ate and ate. The feast lasted for three hours. Luciano patted himself on his belly, belched, and left the table to go to the restroom.

As soon as Masseria was alone at the table, four gunmen—Bugsy Siegel, Vito Genovese, Albert Anastasia, and Joe Adonis—burst into the restaurant. Joe tried to hide but couldn't avoid the path of six bullets, at least one of which killed him.

Another 14 slugs tore up the restaurant wall behind Masseria. Luciano came out of the restroom and left the restaurant before

⚲ MEYER LANSKY

Meyer Lansky may have been the most powerful mobster ever, and, contrary to the stereotype, he wasn't Italian. He was Polish and Jewish, and had been born with the name Maier Suchowljansky. Lansky never had to commit a violent act on his own.[12] That was because his right-hand man, Bugsy Siegel, was a brutal psychopath. Lansky left the strong-arm stuff to others.[13]

He was a businessman, and he made tremendous amounts of money. He took longtime mob activities and made them bigger. For example, instead of putting small gambling parlors in the back rooms of social clubs, Lansky built Las Vegas. Even after Bugsy Siegel, who had been in charge of Las Vegas, was whacked in Los Angeles in 1947, Lansky continued to make money hand over fist.[14]

When the government tried in 1970 to get Lansky the same way they'd gotten Al Capone, by proving that he was guilty of tax evasion, Lansky fled to Israel and waited until the heat was off. He returned to the United States and died of natural causes, a rich man, in 1983.[15]

the police arrived. For the four gunmen, it wasn't a silky smooth getaway. When the driver stalled the car, Bugsy slugged him, but everyone escaped anyway.[16]

BIG PAULIE'S LAST RIDE

Paul Castellano was born on June 26, 1915, in the Bensonhurst section of Brooklyn and was a capo in the Gambino crime family for an amazing 38 years, from 1938–76. Big Paulie was the son of a butcher who, using corrupt techniques, had become a multimillionaire in the meatpacking business. He was not a popular man with most of the soldiers in the crime family. Aloof, he considered himself above many of the crimes that had made him so rich. He did not like to get his hands dirty.

When he was named boss of the family after Carlo Gambino's death in 1976, many members of the family, including John Gotti, were irritated because they felt Paulie got the job because he was Don Carlo's brother-in-law. They felt the new godfather should have been Aneillo Dellacroce, who had served as Don Carlo's underboss since 1965.

During his last days, Gambino had said that no new made men would be initiated. The family, he felt, was big enough. If they needed outside help they could hire outside help. As soon as Castellano took over, this rule was abolished, and new members were initiated left and right. These new members included Sammy "The Bull" Gravano and John Gotti.

The beginning of the end for Castellano came in 1983 when the FBI placed a bug in his kitchen and listened in on conferences Paulie held with his underlings. Using the resulting tapes as evidence, Castellano was charged by the feds with 78 counts of car theft, 25 murders, cocaine dealing, extortion, prostitution, and racketeering.

John Gotti was already furious at Castellano over the charges but lost it after Deallacroce died from natural causes on December 2, 1985. Paulie Castellano had to go.

Castellano came to a bad end, full of lead, lying on a Manhattan street. At 6:00 in the evening on December 16, 1985, Manhattan was hustling and bustling with Christmas shoppers. On East 46th Street, not far from Third Avenue, Big Paulie pulled up in a Lincoln in front of Sparks Steak House, where he planned to eat dinner. Waiting for him on the street were four men in white coats,

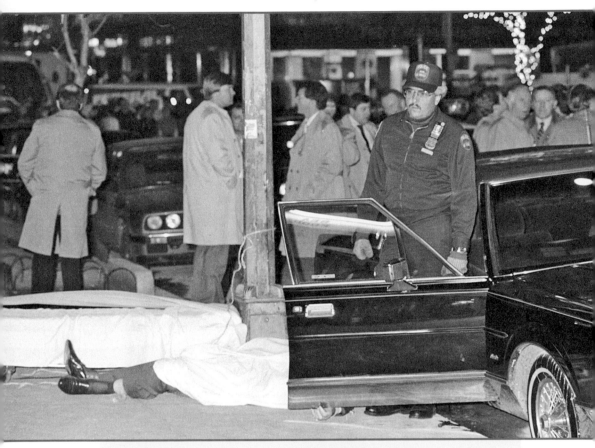

The covered body of crime boss Paul C. Castellano after he and his driver were gunned down outside Sparks Steak House on December 16, 1985. *Bettmann/Corbis*

all holding walkie-talkies. Another man observed from across the street. Three more watched from down the block.

John Gotti, the soon-to-be boss, and Sammy Gravano were in a car on the other side of Third. The last member of the team was stationed inside the restaurant. When Castellano and his driver, Tommy Bilotti, got out of the Lincoln, Castellano was shot first. Terrified, Bilotti tried to get back in the car but didn't make it. He was shot dead as well. Gotti and Gravano then cruised slowly past the scene to make sure that Castellano and Bilotti didn't move. Gotti became boss and Gravano became his right-hand man.[17]

That's the way it goes in mob land. Mobsters worry more about being murdered by other mobsters than they do about getting arrested by the police and going to prison.

The murder of Paul Castellano was also one of the few mob rubouts that led to an arrest and a successful prosecution. The murder of Big Paulie was among the charges brought against John Gotti, and one of the reasons he was eventually sent to prison for the rest of his life.

When the
Government
Declares War

When a crime problem as large as organized crime plagues a nation, individual criminal investigations and the occasional arrest aren't enough to stop the criminals. During the early 1960s the United States government decided to go to war with the Italian mob. President John F. Kennedy's (JFK) brother, Attorney General Robert Kennedy, wanted to make the Mafia a prime target of Justice Department resources. Robert Kennedy, however, got no help from the FBI in this effort because the head of the FBI, J. Edgar Hoover, still denied that there was any such thing as a national crime syndicate. Robert's main target was organized-crime involvement in labor unions. Specifically, he targeted Jimmy Hoffa, head of the Teamsters, one of the nation's largest labor unions. Kennedy tormented Hoffa, forcing him to testify on television in front of a national audience.[1] Kennedy gathered evidence against Sam Giancana, head of Chicago's Outfit but was unable to come up with enough to arrest him.[2] He had the mob boss in New Orleans, Carlos Marcello, deported.[3]

In the meantime, there were members of organized crime who felt betrayed by the Kennedy brothers. Their father, Joseph P. Kennedy, had made much of his riches selling bootleg liquor, working side by side with members of organized crime.[4] When Joseph Kennedy sensed that his son, John, was going to have difficulty beating Richard Nixon to win the 1960 presidential election, mobsters "fixed" the election in key districts of Illinois and perhaps swung

As Attorney General, Robert Kennedy led the fight against organized crime during the early 1960s. *Steve Schapiro/Corbis*

the balance in favor of Kennedy in what turned out to be a very close election.[5] Now Robert was hassling organized crime. It was ungrateful and irritating.

Another reason organized crime was upset with President Kennedy was that he had failed to kick the Communists out of Cuba. The mob had owned and operated many moneymaking gambling casinos in Cuba until Fidel Castro took over the island nation. Castro kicked the mobsters out. Since organized crime saw Kennedy as owing them a favor, they wondered why he didn't invade Cuba, kick out Castro, and let the mob have their casinos back. One of the casino owners, Santos Trafficante, was imprisoned in Cuba for a time by Castro, and, when he was released and allowed to return to the United States, he became a target of Robert Kennedy's anti-mob investigations.[6]

Robert's anti-mob offensive, which did no measurable harm to organized-crime business, came to an end on November 22, 1963, when his brother was shot and killed during a parade through Dallas, Texas. Was organized crime responsible for JFK's death? Though it cannot be proved, it remains a possibility.

After President Kennedy was assassinated in Dallas in 1963, Mafia leaders behaved suspiciously, sometimes bragging about being involved in the president's death, and sparking rumors that the mob had killed Kennedy in retaliation for his brother's activities.

One of the mob leaders most frequently mentioned as a suspect in the presidential assassination is Carlos Marcello. Marcello was born Calogero Minacero and became the boss of America's oldest Mafia family, based in New Orleans, Louisiana. He was a crime boss during the 1950s, '60s and '70s. During that time, Marcello's power spread from New Orleans westward and by the time of President Kennedy's assassination, it encompassed Dallas.

Marcello was furious with the Kennedys after Attorney General Robert Kennedy had him deported in April 1961. Robert Kennedy had discovered that Marcello had a fake birth certificate that listed his place of birth as Guatemala. Since he had never legally emigrated from there to the United States, Kennedy ordered Marcello deported. This was just a technicality. The real reason for deporting him was that he was a high-ranking member of organized crime. Marcello was "kidnapped" (his word) and flown to Guatemala without being allowed to even make a phone call. While in Latin

America, Marcello had a hellish experience, wandering for several days in the jungle with a broken rib. He flew back to the United States four months later, according to the U.S. Border Patrol.

After his return, Marcello reportedly said of the Kennedys, "Take the stone out of my shoe." This meant he wanted the thing that was irritating him to be removed.

After his return his lawyers demanded that he be given a court hearing to determine his immigration status. That hearing concluded on November 22, 1963, the very day that President Kennedy was assassinated. Marcello was found not guilty of illegal immigration and was not deported.

Years later, as part of an FBI sting called BRILAB (short for "bribery and labor"), the FBI made 1,350 tapes of Marcello's conversations between February 1979 and February 1980. On the tapes Marcello thought he was talking to wiseguys, but he was actually talking to FBI moles. When Marcello was eventually arrested on racketeering charges, the judge refused to allow the tapes to be played in court.[7]

According to former Chief Counsel of the House Select Committee on Assassinations, and the man who wrote the RICO laws, G. Robert Blakey, Marcello "implicated himself in the assassination on three of those tapes . . . On one tape, Marcello asked the other person to leave the room and resume the conversation in the secrecy of his car when the assassination came up. Marcello said something like, 'We don't talk about that in here.'"

Las Vegas private investigator Ed Becker says Marcello told him in September 1962 about a plan to assassinate President Kennedy, which included the using of a "nut" to deflect blame from the mob. The official version of the JFK assassination is that the president was murdered by Lee Harvey Oswald, a lone deranged individual.

Frank Ragano was, for 27 years, the lawyer for Florida mob boss Santos Trafficante. For 15 of those years he also represented Teamster president Jimmy Hoffa. In 1992 Ragano revealed knowledge of a plot involving Hoffa, Trafficante, and Marcello to assassinate the president. All three men are dead now, but at the time of Ragano's statement Marcello was still alive, in jail, where he reportedly was suffering from Alzheimer's disease. Ragano said he became an "unwitting intermediary" to the plot when he met with Hoffa at Teamsters headquarters in Washington, D.C., in

Reputed mob leader Carlos Marcello leaves federal court in New
Orleans during the FBI's BRILAB investigation in December 1980.
Bettmann/Corbis

January or February 1963. Ragano, who was about to fly to New Orleans for a meeting with Trafficante and Marcello, says Hoffa told him, "Tell Marcello and Trafficante they have to kill the president."

Ragano continued, "Hoffa said to me, 'This has to be done.' Jimmy was ranting and raving for a long time. I didn't take it seriously because I knew Jimmy was a hothead with a short attention span. Marcello and Trafficante never met Hoffa. I had lawyer-client privilege with Hoffa and Trafficante, so I was made go-between. Marcello and Trafficante were extremely cautious. They always wanted to be able to truthfully say they never met Hoffa."

Ragano claims he met with Trafficante and Marcello at the Royal Orleans Hotel a few days later.

Ragano continued, "I told them, 'You won't believe what Hoffa wants me to tell you. Jimmy wants you to kill the president.' They didn't laugh. . . . Their looks scared me. It made me think they already had such a thought in mind."

Ragano says he returned to Washington, D.C., told Hoffa he had delivered the message and Hoffa reportedly replied, "It is going to be done."

On November 22, 1963, Hoffa called Ragano three or four minutes after the first news bulletins.

"Have you heard the good news?" Hoffa asked. "They killed the S.O.B. This means Bobby is out as Attorney General."

The House Select Committee concluded that "Marcello had the motive, means and opportunity to have President John F. Kennedy assassinated." However, they wrote, they found no direct evidence linking Marcello with the assassination.

Although no direct evidence was found, some interesting coincidences exist to suggest organized crime could have been involved. Oswald, the official assassin, had an uncle named Dutz Murret who worked for Marcello. Oswald's mother had dated men who worked for Marcello. Two days after the assassination Oswald himself was murdered by Jack Ruby, a Dallas strip-club owner with a background in organized crime.

FBI agent Joseph Hauser went undercover in 1979 to investigate Marcello's crime organization. According to Hauser, Marcello admitted to knowing Oswald and his uncle, Charles "Dutz" Murret, and that Oswald worked for him in 1963 as a runner for his betting operation.

There is other evidence. A report from an FBI informant says that Oswald once received money from a Marcello underboss in a restaurant owned by Marcello's brother, Joseph.

In 1980 Hauser talked to Carlos' brother, Joseph, about the way the Kennedys had hassled him and his brother during the early 1960s. Joseph Marcello reportedly replied, "Don't worry, we took care of them, didn't we?"

Another suspect in President Kennedy's death was Florida Mafia boss Santos Trafficante, who was based in Tampa and controlled mob operations in Cuba before Castro's revolution ousted the old government and threw the mob out of the country. Trafficante had also had his operation disrupted by Robert Kennedy's anti-mob war. The story gets complicated by the fact that the CIA was using mobsters as spies to gather information inside Cuba, and to, if possible, assassinate Cuban dictator Fidel Castro. So Robert Kennedy's war was getting in the way of a CIA operation, a simple case of the government's right hand not knowing what the left hand was doing.

Trafficante died following triple-bypass surgery in 1987 in Houston, Texas. On his death bed, he told his lawyer, Frank Ragano, "Marcello [messed] up. We should not have killed John. We should have killed Bobby." Ragano believed this was a reference to the Kennedy brothers.

The third most frequently discussed Mafia suspect in the presidential assassination was Chicago mob boss Sam Giancana. In the early 1960s Giancana helped the CIA (with money and personnel) in covert operations within Cuba to rid that country of Castro.

In 1988 Judith Exner, who was a mistress to both Giancana and JFK, told *People* magazine, "I lied when I said that President Kennedy was unaware of my friendship with mobsters. He knew everything about my dealings with Sam Giancana and Johnny Roselli because I was seeing them for him."

Giancana was a braggart. The FBI learned of CIA/Mafia plans to assassinate Castro in 1960, when Giancana spilled the beans.

According to Giancana's half-brother Chuck in his book *Double Cross*, President Kennedy was murdered by a team of Chicago hitmen sent to Dallas by Giancana. Although there is no outside evidence to support this claim, a House Select Committee did come to the conclusion that other members of organized crime (namely Carlos Marcello, Jimmy Hoffa, and Santo Trafficante) had the "motive, means and opportunity" to kill President Kennedy.[8]

And so, there was a time, about 45 years ago, when the Italian mob was so powerful in the United States that they could brag about killing the leader of the free world and people believed—and still do today—that it was possible.

A Brief History of the Gambino Crime Family

Though crime families exist around the world, one of the most famous, the Gambino family, is headquartered in New York City. It is a typical crime family, both in its structure and in its struggles against the authorities. Law enforcement has attacked the Gambino family with all of the techniques at their disposal: informants, moles, surveillance, and new laws.

DON CARLO

Carlo Gambino was born in Sicily in 1902, a member of an organized crime family. He was by birthright a member of The Honored Society, later known as the Mafia. Gambino committed his first murders for the society as a teenager and was officially initiated as a **made man** at the age of 19 in 1921. With Benito Mussolini's fascist regime in power in Italy, Gambino crossed the Atlantic Ocean in a shipping boat, eating and drinking nothing, it is said, but anchovies and wine. He entered the United States as an illegal alien. In the United States he lived with his cousins, the Castellanos. He never became a U.S. citizen, but rather was granted political refugee status.[1]

Like other mobsters of the era, Gambino and his cousins went into the illegal-booze business during Prohibition. Carlo was very close to his cousin, another up-and-coming made man, Big Paulie Castellano. The pair married each other's sisters. Carlo was also a "gun for hire," a professional killer, who'd work for whomever wanted to pay for his services. He worked mostly, however, for Lucky Luciano, who was found guilty of running a prostitution ring in 1936 and deported back to Italy during the 1940s.[2]

The organization Carlo worked for, with Luciano out of the picture, was led by Albert Anastasia. Anastasia, who was cruel and unpredictable, was murdered in a barber's chair in 1957. Gambino orchestrated the kill, and although he didn't fire any of the shots, was in the basement of the hotel when the hit took place. The crime family after that was led by Vito Genovese—and Gambino was underboss.[3]

Genovese's stock in trade was heroin. The feds—who at that time were not at war with organized crime but were in a war against drugs—finally caught up with Genovese and sent Vito to jail for drug trafficking. Gambino became the leader of the organization, and this is the reason why, for the rest of his life, he believed that La Cosa Nostra should stay away from drug dealing.

Gambino took over the leadership of the organization, which quickly became known as the Gambino crime family, a name it still goes by today, almost 30 years after Don Carlo's death. Gambino operated during J. Edgar Hoover's reign as the head of the FBI. It was a good time for organized crime. Hoover, publicly at least, stated that he didn't believe the Mafia existed. So it was unlikely that federal agents were going to cause La Cosa Nostra any major problems.

Gambino died of a heart attack in 1976, at the age of 74. Not many hoodlums die of old age. Don Carlo was lucky in a couple of ways. Old men in the mob often have spent more than half of their lives behind bars, but not Gambino. The truth was, he had spent less than two years in jail—for selling bootleg liquor—and that was when he was young.

One of the reasons Gambino stayed out of trouble was that he was even-tempered. Though he was a killer as a teenager, later in his life he was not a directly violent man. He could order a man's murder without feeling a pang of guilt, but he would not commit murder himself. Back in those days it was difficult to prosecute a mob boss such as Gambino who separated himself from the crimes his organization committed. Later, the RICO laws made it easier

Gangster Carlo Gambino in a mug shot. *Bettmann/Corbis*

to put mob bosses behind bars. Gambino was also among the first mobsters to realize that the FBI had recording devices planted everywhere. Therefore, he learned to speak in code, making himself understood to his underlings without providing the feds anything they could use to arrest him. And finally, he was a master at bribing officials. Whenever it looked like he was headed for trouble with the law, he knew just which politician or judge to bribe, and his problems went away.[4]

As godfather, Don Carlo spread his moneymaking organization into the nooks and crannies of New York City commerce. Shipping, trucking, and garbage collection in New York City all operated under Don Carlo's thumb.

Gambino's last move as godfather was instructing his capos to elect his cousin, Paul Castellano, as his successor. That move led to Castellano's murder and the takeover of the family by John Gotti.[5]

Today, the section of Manhattan most associated with Italy is called "Little Italy," and is in the lower portion of the island, south of Greenwich Village. But that was not the case during the mid-twentieth century when John Gotti was a child. At that time the largest cluster of Italian-Americans in Manhattan was in what was then known as Italian Harlem, in the northeastern section of the island. It was in Italian Harlem that John first saw mobsters, and he was impressed from the beginning. In 1950, when John was 10, his family moved to Sheepshead Bay, Brooklyn. A year later, they moved again, this time to the East New York section of Brooklyn, where the Mafia was in control.

The godfather of the mob at that time was Albert Anastasia. Not that anyone in East New York ever saw him. He lived in a large house in New Jersey and allowed his capos and soldiers to do the dirty work for him. Anastasia was a cruel man who seemingly enjoyed punishing those who didn't bow before the power of La Cosa Nostra. More visible in John's new neighborhood was one of Anastasia's most trusted men, Carlo Gambino.

Adult mobsters in East New York often delegated menial tasks to thuggish youths, thus creating a sort of farm system for the development of future hoodlums. Peter Gotti, John's older brother, was the first of the Gotti boys to join a gang of mob wannabes. John's younger brother, Richard, soon joined the gang as well. John followed suit in 1952, and the three Gotti brothers beat up those who wouldn't play ball and ran errands for the neighborhood wise-guys. The Gotti boys didn't like school and their parents were too busy trying to get by to care if their sons were running wild. John quit school at 16 so he could work full time for the adult mob. Soon thereafter, he became leader of the Fulton-Rockaway Boys. They stole cars, rolled drunks, and fenced stolen goods.[6]

As the godfather of the Gambino family in later years, John Gotti became known as "The Teflon Don" because the legal system had trouble putting him away. He seemed to slip away from trouble. This was a trait that developed early for Johnny Boy. Between 1957 and 1961, Gotti was arrested five times—yet he never had to serve any jail time. In each case, the charges were either dropped or the sentence reduced to probation.

During the early 1960s Gotti married and had kids. Mob headquarters at that time was near JFK airport, and John was put to work impersonating an airport worker and stealing truckloads of merchandise as they arrived at the airport on cargo planes.[7]

Other criminal activities put in place at that time involved loansharking and **bookmaking**, taking advantage of the many saloons in the neighborhood. Joining the operation at this point was John's younger brother, Gene, and Salvatore Ruggiero, the younger brother of John Gotti's childhood friend and later his secretary, Angelo "Quack-Quack" Ruggiero. It was hijacking trucks that earned John—along with Quack-Quack and John's brother, Gene—his first trip to prison. The threesome was caught stealing a truck filled with women's dresses at the airport. Following the arrest, witnesses to past hijackings identified photos of John and Quack-Quack and a second charge was added to their indictment. Despite the double charges, however, John and Quack-Quack only served three years in prison (1969–72) at the United States penitentiary in Lewisburg, Pennsylvania. A friendly judge in Queens ruled that the evidence in the second charge had been gathered illegally.

After prison, Gotti picked up where he'd left off. He did not report directly to Gambino, but rather to Don Carlo's underboss, Aniello Dellacroce, who quickly became a father figure to Gotti. Dellacroce was arrested in 1972 on tax evasion charges, convicted, and sent to prison for a year. It would be six years before he got out, however, as a second charge of failing to testify, despite being granted immunity, was tagged on after he was in prison. After that, Gotti reported directly to Gambino. When Gambino died and left his cousin Paul Castellano in charge, Gotti's ambition took over. Gotti had Castellano murdered in 1985 and took over the family. His rise through the ranks had been meteoric. He'd only been an officially made man since 1977.

◊ THE MAFIA INDUCTION CEREMONY

Like many other secret societies, the Mafia holds secret ceremonies when it is inducting new members into the fold. When a hood became a made man, an official member of his crime family, he was initiated in a dark room lit only by flickering candles. The head of the family conducted the ceremony and everyone dressed in black suits, as they might dress if they were attending a funeral.

"You are to be inducted into the honored society of Cosa Nostra," the godfather said. The inductee must pledge loyalty to the family. He must pledge to put the interests of the crime family above his own, and above those of his own family—that is, his wife and children. The final pledge was considered the most important. He had to pledge that, if ordered, he would kill. Blood from the inductee's finger was rubbed onto a holy card and the card was set afire. The inductee then pledged *omerta*: that he would always keep the business of Cosa Nostra secret. Revealing the activities of the group would result, he was told, in his soul burning like that holy card.[8]

During the 1980s the FBI was eager to put Gotti behind bars. Not only was he a mobster, but he also liked publicity. He dressed well, in Armani suits, and never shied away from a reporter's camera. The FBI felt like Gotti was rubbing law enforcement's noses in his mob success. In 1987 Gotti was tried on RICO charges but, after a long trial that dominated the newspapers, he was acquitted by a jury. Evidence later surfaced that jurors had been bribed by Gotti to find him not guilty. Two other court cases followed in state courtrooms and Gotti walked away from them as well. In one an eyewitness, no doubt thinking of his own safety, refused to identify Gotti in court.[9] During this time Gotti became the first mobster/media superstar.

In 1989 Gotti's luck began to run out. A combined force of FBI agents and New York City police went after Gotti using a three-pronged attack. Their strategy involved:

1. Sharp detective work
2. Electronic surveillance
3. The testimony of a key informant[10]

The FBI bugged a room over a social club where they knew Gotti held secret meetings. The FBI tapes caught Gotti admitting to at least three murders. Sammy Gravano, one of Gotti's right-

John Gotti on trial for murder in New York Supreme Court in Manhattan, NY, on January 20, 1990. *Richard Drew/AP*

hand men, ratted him out and new RICO charges were filed against the Teflon Don. This time the case was airtight, and the jury was protected from threats and bribes. In 1992 Gotti was convicted and sentenced to life in prison. He died of cancer behind bars at the age of 61.[11]

In this day and age, when mobsters take their vows of omerta lightly and rat out their superiors on a regular basis, it is doubtful that any future mobster will be able to enjoy the kind of fame and riches that Gotti experienced before the FBI finally caught up with him.

THE MOLE

The biggest bust of Gambino mobsters was the result of an undercover agent who worked his way inside the family's ranks. That bust took place in 2005. In that case 31 mobsters, including the reputed head of the family, Arnold "Zeke" Squiltieri, were arrested. The busts were the result of an undercover FBI agent—whose name was never released to the public—who worked his way inside the organization by pretending to be a trustworthy associate. He gathered information that the family was still involved in extortion, loan-sharking, gambling, and other crimes.

According to U.S. attorney David Kelley, the agent "risked his life as a mole for the better part of two years" to gather the evidence leading to the arrests. The mole was about to be made a made man and be officially inducted into the Mafia when the busts were made. The agent was proof that "Donnie Brascos" are still out there. The lesson to mobsters was clear: Trust no one.[12]

In 2008 the boom came down again on the Gambinos, with all of the high-ranking members of the organization, both in the United States and in Italy, being arrested at the same time—more than 60 mobsters in all. This time, however, law enforcement was quiet about how the evidence was gathered, but suspicion was that another undercover agent had pulled off a successful mission.[13]

Chronology

1890–1914   In the two decades leading up to World War I, hundreds of thousands of Italians immigrate to the United States, including a handful familiar in the ways of the Mafia. In Europe each crime organization would have its own turf, the boundaries of which would be understood by all. In order to be in the Sicilian Mafia you had to be from Sicily. But, once in America these lines blurred and new geographical divisions arise—the city, the borough, the neighborhood. The most common organized crime of the period is "Black Hand" extortion. In 1924, the Black Hand is still being referred to by the American press as "the backbone of the Mafia."[1]

1920   Start of Prohibition. With the ratification of the 18th Amendment it becomes illegal to make, distribute, possess, or drink alcoholic beverages—thus creating millions of criminals who were, the day before, law-abiding citizens. The illegal-booze racket becomes huge. Political corruption skyrockets and violence grows as criminals fight relentless turf battles for control.

1927–31   After a series of whackings known as the Castellimarese Wars, Lucky Luciano takes over as "Boss of Bosses."

1930   Release of the movie *Little Caesar*, starring Edward G. Robinson as Rico Bandello. The movie shows the psychology behind organized crime, the opportunity it gives some men for wealth and power outside the system. The film also portrays government and law enforcement as corrupt, putting a gray area between the guys in the white hats and the guys in the black hats. Isn't Rico only doing what legitimate officials are doing, only out in the open?

1929   *February 14:* The St. Valentine's Day Massacre. Organized crime in Chicago comes under Italian control, with Al Capone running the show.

1931   The whacking of Mafia leaders Joseph Masseria and Salvatore Maranzano brings about the Commission, an inter-family group to oversee Mafia affairs.

1931   Following an investigation and arrest by Eliot Ness and "The Untouchables," along with the IRS, Al Capone is convicted of tax evasion and sentenced to 11 years in prison.

1933   *December 5:* The 21st Amendment to the Constitution is ratified, repealing Prohibition. With alcohol once again legal, many mobsters have to find another line of work. Gangsters keep a lower profile and less is written about the problems of organized crime in the newspapers.

1937   Lucky Luciano is removed from power by law enforcement.

1940   *November:* George McLane becomes the first mobster to invoke his Fifth Amendment right against self-incrimination to avoid testifying.

1941–45   The U.S. military seeks out and receives the aid of the Mafia in liberating Sicily and Italy from the Axis powers.

1950–51   *May 10–September 1:* The Special Committee to Investigate Organized Crime in Interstate Commerce, helmed by Senator Estes Kefauver, hears testimony about organized narcotics trafficking and syndicated gambling. The hearings expose the relationship between political corruption and organized crime and are broadcast live on radio and television. The hearings force the FBI to change its "no such thing as the Mafia" stance. Although few new anti-mob laws came out of the hearings, there was a tremendous growth in the public's anti-mob feelings.

1957   The Bust at Apalachin. At a meeting of the Commission, with all the major families represented, 58 are arrested. It is now almost impossible to claim, as had often been done, that the Mafia did not exist.

1957–60 The Senate Rackets Committee holds hearings and the public learns for the first time of the association between organized crime and the leaders of major U.S. labor unions.

1957–64 A massive intelligence-gathering operation is carried out by the FBI, much of it including illegal wiretaps and buggings.

1961–63 With Robert Kennedy as the U.S. Attorney General, the Justice Department declares war on the Mafia.

1961 *April:* Attorney General Robert Kennedy has mob boss Carlos Marcello deported. Marcello is in charge of organized-crime activities from New Orleans to Dallas.

1963 America learns what a canary is—as well as the structure of La Cosa Nostra and the names of its leaders—when Joseph Valachi, a Mafia soldier with a great memory for details, sings and sings and sings to a U.S. Senate committee.

1963 *November 22:* John F. Kennedy is assassinated in Dallas, Texas, and Lyndon Johnson becomes the new president, effectively ending the government's war on organized crime.

1968 Omnibus Crime Control Act. After recommendations by a presidential commission, Congress passes the Omnibus Crime Control Act, which gives law enforcement greater power to combat the Mafia. New powers include authorized wiretapping.

1970 RICO laws passed by Congress. The set of laws allow law enforcement to arrest mobsters who are part of a conspiracy to commit a crime.

1976 FBI agent Joe Pistone gets inside the Bonanno family

1976 *September 17:* The House Select Committee on Assassinations releases the results of its investigation into the assassination of President Kennedy. The committee concludes that they can find no evidence that the Mafia as an organization was behind President Kennedy's death, but that there is a possibility that individuals involved with organized crime "may have been involved."

1980–2000   Using RICO laws, a massive assault by the FBI cripples the mob. Many Mafia heads are convicted of racketeering or murder and put in prison.

2008   Mafia families continue to operate in New York and Chicago, and smaller, less-powerful groups remain in other cities.

Endnotes

Introduction

1. American Local History Network, "John Murel and the Mystic Clan," *The Past Whispers*. http://www.thepastwhispers.com/ALHN_Murel.html.
2. Joseph Geringer, "Jean Lafitte: Gentleman Pirate of New Orleans," Crime Library. http://www.crimelibrary.com.
3. Selwyn Raab, *Five Families* (New York: St. Martin's Press, 2006), 5, 135.
4. Raab, 691.
5. "Seven Massacred in Chicago Beer War," *The Daily News* February 15, 1929, 1, 2.
6. Gus Russo, *The Outfit* (New York: Bloomsbury, 2001), 2.

Chapter 1

1. Raab, 104.

Chapter 2

1. Raab, 228.
2. Raab, 229.
3. John Simeone and David Jacobs, *The Complete Idiot's Guide to the FBI* (New York: Alpha Books, 2003).
4. Raab, 24.
5. Raab, 602.
6. Raab, 268.
7. Raab, 228.
8. Bill Bickel, "The Way of the Wiseguy: An Interview With 'Donnie Brasco,'" *Crime Justice & America* (Winter 2004/5). http://www.crime-week.com/cja/0904brasco.html.
9. Simeone, 122.
10. FBI official Web site. http://www.fbi.gov/hq/cid/orgcrime/aboutocs.htm.
11. Ibid.
12. Ibid.

Chapter 3

1. Jerry Capeci, *The Complete Idiot's Guide to the Mafia* (New York: Alpha Books, 2002).
2. "Genovese La Cosa Nostra Family," FBI Web site. http://www.fbi.gov.
3. Raab, 135.
4. Raab, 202.
5. Raab, 137.
6. Ibid.
7. John H. Davis, *Mafia Dynasty* (New York: HarperTorch, 1993), 427–428.
8. Raab, 436–438.
9. Arnold H. Lubasch, "Gravano Insists He Was Loyal Soldier," *New York Times*, March 13, 1992.
10. Capeci, 261.
11. ABC News, "Fourteen reputed mobsters indicted in 'Operation Family Secrets'." http://www.abcnews.com.

12. Randy Bergmann, "Brooklyn's heavy accent: New York borough has left its mark on American culture," *Arizona Republic* (June 2, 2002). Associated Press dispatch. http://www.olgaa.com/Baseball/Tournaments/tourney_11yrold_ws_brooklyn.htm.

13. ABC News, "Fourteen reputed mobsters indicted in 'Operation Family Secrets.'" http://www.abcnews.com. Posted April 25, 2005.

Chapter 4

1. Davis, 192.

2. Raab, 135.

3. Nick Pisa, "Your Time Has Come," *New York Post* Online. http:// www.nypost.com.

4. Ibid.

5. Frances D'Emilio, "Sordid Chapter in Corleone's History Ends," *Newsday* Online. http://www.newsday.com.

Chapter 5

1. Jerry Capeci, "This Week in Gangland: The Online Column," *Gangland News* Online. http://www.ganglandnews.com.

2. Raab, 724.

3. Davis, *Mafia Dynasty*, 92–94.

4. David H. Jacobs, *The Mafia's Greatest Hits* (New York: Citadel Press, 2006), 186.

Chapter 6

1. "Famous Cases: Alphonse Capone, aka. Al, Scarface," FBI Web site. http://www.fbi.gov/libref/historic/famcases/capone/capone.htm.

2. Capeci, *Complete Idiot's Guide*, 82.

3. Raab, 214, 578, 693.

4. Gerard E. Lynch, "RICO: The Crime of Being a Criminal," *Columbia Law Review* 661 (1987). http://www.ipsn.org/court_cases/rico-crime_of_being_a_criminal.htm.

5. G. Robert Blakey and Richard N. Billings, *The Plot to Kill the President: Organized Crime Assassinated JFK* (New York: Times Books, 1981).

6. Michael Benson, *Who's Who in the JFK Assassination: An A to Z Encyclopedia* (New York: Citadel, 1998), 41–42.

7. "But Who's Really The Boss?" Crime Library. http://www.crimelibrary.com.

Chapter 7

1. Alex Ginsberg, "Russian Mobsters Nailed in '92 Slays," *New York Post* Online. http://www.nypost.com.

2. Ibid.

3. Michael Benson, *Inside Secret Societies* (New York: Citadel Press, 2005), 243.

4. Ning-Ning Mahlmann, "Chinese Criminal Enterprises." http://www.usinfo.state.gov/eap/Archive_Index/Chinese_Criminal_Enterprises.html.

5. Hong Kong government Web site. http://www.sc.info.gov.hk/gb/www.police.gov.hk/review/2002/html/text/t_e_region.htm.

6. Benson, *Inside Secret Societies*, 222–223.

7. "Facts and Figures 2003: Organized Crime," FBI Web site. http://www.fbi.gov/libref/factsfigure/orgcrime.htm.
8. Benson, *Inside Secret Societies*, 72.

Chapter 8

1. Jacobs, 131–155.
2. T.J. English, *Paddywhacked: The Untold Story of the Irish American Gangster* (New York: Regan Books, 2005), 132–133, 181–182.
3. "Diamond is Slain After Acquittal," *Brooklyn Daily Eagle*, December 18, 1931, 1.
4. "As Galante Died 20 Mob Bosses Hailed Slaying," *Daily News*, July 15, 1979, 1, 3.
5. Jacobs, 185–202.
6. Michael Benson, *Encyclopedia of the JFK Assassination* (New York: Checkmark Books, 2002), 93–94.
7. Ibid.
8. Jacobs, 156–184.
9. "Deep Six For Johnny," *Time* magazine, August 23, 1976; Benson, *Encyclopedia*, 224.
10. Russo, 144–145.
11. Gus Russo, *The Outfit* (New York: Bloomsbury Books, 2001), 294.
12. Jacobs, 103–130.
13. Raab, 100–101.
14. Jacobs, 37–53.
15. Jacobs, 203–221.
16. Jacobs, 37–53.
17. Jacobs, 203–221.

Chapter 9

1. Russo, 313.
2. Ibid., 83.
3. Ibid., 410.

4. Ibid., 358–362
5. Ibid., 400–401.
6. Benson, *Encyclopedia*, 268.
7. Capeci, *Complete Idiot's Guide*, 107.
8. Benson, *Encyclopedia*, 147–148.

Chapter 10

1. Davis, 20–28.
2. "Luciano and Eight Found Guilty," *Daily News*, June 8, 1936, 1, 3.
3. Davis, 77–80.
4. Davis, 296.
5. Davis, 169–70.
6. Davis, 68–70.
7. Davis, 110–112.
8. Capeci, *Complete Idiot's Guide*, 20–21.
9. Richard Pyle, "John Gotti, the Dapper Don, dies behind bars at 61," *Boston Globe*, June 10, 2002. http://www.boston.com/news/daily/10/gotti.htm.
10. "John Gotti: How We Made the Charges Stick," FBI Web site. http://www.fbi.gov/page2/april07/gotti040207.htm.
11. Davis, 306–308, 368–373.
12. Fox News, "Alleged Gambino Boss, 30 Others Arrested." http://www.FoxNews.com.
13. Jonathan Dienst, Joseph Valiquette, and Alice McQuillan, "Reputed Mobsters Busted in Major Roundup." http://www.wnbc.com.

Chronology

1. "Black Hand Broken Here," *Pittsburgh Post*, October 14, 1924, 1, 2.

Glossary

bookmaking Illegally taking bets.

bootlegging The manufacture, distribution and sale of illegal alcoholic beverages.

capo Mob lieutenant.

espionage Use of undercover agents to learn information (called intelligence) or sabotage the efforts of the other organization.

godfather Leader of an Italian organized crime family.

loan-sharking Illegally lending money and charging large interest fees; people late in paying back their loans are beat up by mob goons.

made man Official member of La Cosa Nostra.

omerta Mafia code of silence.

RICO Laws Laws designed to combat Racketeer Influenced and Corrupt Organizations.

skim Percentage of income taken from businesses by organized crime in exchange for "protection"; or what a business owner pays to the mob to avoid something bad happening.

Bibliography

Adams, Cindy. "Word from wiseguy." *New York Post*, October 18, 2004, p. 20.

Benson, Michael. *Encyclopedia of the JFK Assassination*. New York: Checkmark Books, 2002.

_____. *Inside Secret Societies*. New York: Citadel Press, 2005.

"Black Hand Broken Here." *Pittsburgh Post*, October 14, 1924, p. 1, 2.

Blakey, G. Robert and Richard N. Billings. *The Plot to Kill the President: Organized Crime Assassinated JFK*. New York: Times Books, 1981.

Blum, Howard. *Gangland: How the FBI Broke the Mob*. New York: Simon & Schuster, 1993.

Campanille, Carl. "Don of the Dead: 5 Gambinos to implicate Gotti in slay plot." *New York Post*, October 25, 2004, p. 27.

Capeci, Jerry. *The Complete Idiot's Guide to the Mafia*. New York: Alpha Books, 2002.

Capeci, Jerry. "Gambinos in Free Fall." *Gang Land News*, July 15, 1999.

Capeci, Jerry. "Jerry Capeci's gang land," *Gangland News* Online. Available online. URL: http://www.gangland.news.com/gotti.htm. Accessed on October 7, 2004.

_____. "This Week in Gangland: The Online Column," *Gangland News* Online. Available online. URL: http://www.gangland-news.com. Posted on November 16, 2000.

Capeci, Jerry and Gene Mustain. *Gotti: Rise and Fall*. New York: Onyx True Crime, 1996.

"Caponi and Ten Indicted: Caponi Brothers and 9 Others Are Indicted by Vote Fraud Jury." *The Chicago Evening Post*, July 2, 1926, p. 1.

Coffey, Joseph and Jerry Schmetterer. *The Coffey Files*. New York: St. Martin's Press, 1991.

Corey, Herbert. *Farewell, Mr. Gangster!* New York: D. Appleton-Century Company, Inc., 1936.

Cornell Smith, Kati, L. Celona, and K. Sheehy. "Feds Launch Chilling Hunt For Corpses In Queens Dumping Lot." *New York Post*, October 5, 2004, pp. 2-3.

Davis, John H. *Mafia Dynasty*. New York: HarperTorch, 1993.

"D'Emilio, Frances. "Sordid Chapter in Corleone's History Ends." *Newsday* Online. Available online. URL: http://www.newsday. com. Posted on April 28, 2006.

Dillon, Nancy, and Alison Gendar. "Gotti's widow: Go dig, but my John didn't do it." *Daily News*, October 5, 2004, p. 4–5.

Dunleavy, Steve. "Blood is thinner than water for 'big dig' mob rat." *New York Post*, October 14, 2004, p. 31.

Egan, Cy. "New Angle In Shooting Of Colombo." *New York Post*, July 1, 1971, p. 1.

English, T.J., *Paddywhacked: The Untold Story of the Irish American Gangster*. New York: Regan Books, 2005.

Gage, Nicholas. "Story of Joe Gallo's Murder: 5 in Colombo Gang Implicated." *New York Times*, May 3, 1972, p. 1.

Gendar, Alison, and Adam Lisberg. "Gotti wife on '80 neighbor: Hey, we didn't kill him." *Daily News*, October 8, 2004, p. 7.

Gendar, Alison, J. Marzulli, and A. Lisberg. "Feds' big dig hasn't run its corpse: Investigators seeking buried victims of mob rubouts." *Daily News*, October 10, 2004, p. 16.

"Genovese La Cosa Nostra Family." FBI Web site. Available online. URL: http://www.FBI.gov. Accessed on April 1, 2006.

Geringer, Joseph. "Jean Lafitte: Gentleman Pirate of New Orleans," Crime Library. Available online. URL: http://www.crimelibrary. com. Accessed on December 15, 2006.

Ginsberg, Alex. "Russian Mobsters Nailed in '92 Slays," *New York Post* Online. Available online. URL: http://www.nypost.com. Posted on April 13, 2006.

Ginsberg, Alex. "Wife: Gotti Cut$ Me Off." *New York Post*, September 23, 2004, p. 25.

The Gotti Tapes. New York: Times Books, 1992.

Grove, Lloyd. "Lowdown: Dressing down the Gottis." *Daily News*, September 22, 2004, p. 30.

Hill, Henry, and Gus Russo. *Gangsters and Goodfellas: The Mob, Witness Protection, and Life on the Run*. New York: M. Evans and Company, 2004.

Hutchinson, Bill. "Gotti goon sez he killed canary." *Daily News*, September 1, 2004, p. 26.

Jacobs, David H. *The Mafia's Greatest Hits*. New York: Citadel Press, 2006.

Johnson, Richard, with P. Froelich, and C. Wilson. "Gotti TV worker bowled over." *New York Post*, September 6, 2004, p. 10.

Kadison, Dan, et al. "Hamptons Diary." *New York Post*, September 7, 2004, p. 22.

Lisberg, Adam. "Don wanted his neighbor removed." *Daily News*, October 5, 2004, p. 4–5.

"Luciano and Eight Found Guilty." *Daily News*, June 8, 1936, p. 1, 3.

Maas, Peter. *Underboss: Sammy The Bull Gravano's Story of Life in the Mafia*. New York: HarperCollins, 1997.

Mainelli, John. "Curtis vows to defy Gotti gag order." *New York Post*, October 22, 2004, p. 137.

Marzulli, John. "Sanit worker came clean for FBI sting." *Daily News*, October 27, 2004, p. 14.

Marzulli, John, G. B. Smith, T. El-Ghobashy, and T. Connor. "Digging up Gambino graveyard: Feds sweep down on deserted Queens lot to search for bodies." *Daily News*, October 5, 2004, p. 3.

May, Allen. "John Gotti: The Last Mafia Icon," Crime Library. Available online. URL: http://www.crimclibrary.com/john/johnmain. htm. Accessed on October 7, 2004.

McGurk, K. C. Smith, and C. Campanile. "Underworld Riches: Gotti graveyard bought by condo builder in summer." *New York Post*, October 6, 2004, p. 3.

McPhee, Michele. "Gambino hit man wants all to know he's no rat." *Daily News*, September 15, 2004, p. 12.

"Mob Kingpin, Woman Shot to Death In Auto: Little Augie Pisano, Beauty Queen Killed." *Macon News*, September 26, 1959.

Mollica, Joe. "Sliwa a linguine weenie at Italian fete." *New York Post*, October 25, 2004, p. 27.

Moore, Robert F., L. Williams, and A. Lisberg. "Family ends silence: Son of Gotti neighbor killed by goons hoping body found." *Daily News*, October 6, 2004, p. 7.

Morgan, Spencer. "My New York." *25 Hours*, October 17, 2004, p. 46.

Mustain, Gene, and Jerry Capeci. *Murder Machine: The True Story of Murder, Madness, and the Mafia*. New York: Dutton, 1992.

"New Stars in Town? Crime Family Looks to Change Reputation on Reality TV," ABC News Online. Available online. URL: http://www.abcnews.go.com/sections/2020/Entertainment/2020_Gotti_040806-1.html. Posted on August 6, 2004.

O'Brien, Joseph, and Andris Kurins. *Boss of Bosses*. New York: Simon & Schuster, 1991.

Ortega, Ralph R., and Thomas Zambito. "Sliwa airs curt reply: Won't clam up on mob." *Daily News*, October 22, 2004, p. 31.

Pelleck, Carl J., and William T. Slattery. "Gambino Heir: A Bonanno Man." *New York Post*, October 16, 1976, p. 1, 3.

Pisa, Nick. "Your Time Has Come," *New York Post* Online. Available online. URL: http://www.Nypost.com. Posted on April 24, 2006.

Raab, Selwyn. *Five Families*. New York: Thomas Dunne Books, 2006.

Rashbaum, William K. "F.B.I. Finds Human Bones at a Mob Dig." *New York Times*, October 12, 2004, p. B3.

Rush, George, and Joanna Molloy. "Gotti's siege of Paris averted by Lizzie." *Daily News*, September 7, 2004, p. 30.

Russo, Gus. *The Outfit*. New York: Bloomsbury Books, 2001.

Saggio, Frankie, and Fred Rosen. *Born to the Mob: The True-Life Story of the Only Man to Work in All Five of New York's Mafia Families*. New York: Thunder's Mouth Press, 2004.

"Seven Massacred in Chicago Beer War." *Daily News*, February 15, 1929, p. 1, 2.

Shawcross, Tim. *The War Against the Mafia*. New York: Harper Paperbacks, 1995.

Shifrel, Scott, and Bill Hutchinson. "Pete's wife Gotti work: Takes office job to pay bills." *Daily News*, September 23, 2004, p. 4.

Sifakis, Carl. *The Mafia Encyclopedia*. New York: Checkmark Books, 1999.

Simeone, John, and David Jacobs. *The Complete Idiot's Guide to the FBI*. New York: Alpha Books, 2003.

Smith, Greg B. "Albanian 'Mafiosi' in Feds' Net." *Daily News*, November 1, 2004, p. 24.

Smith, Kati Cornell, "Gotti's 'clan' rocked: 'Genius' busted." *New York Post*, September 30, 2004, p. 20.

Smith, Kati Cornell, Hasani Gittens, Murray Weiss, and Gersh Kuntzman. "The Bone-Annos: Two capos' remains dug up in Gambinos' Queens graveyard." *New York Post*, October 13, 2004, p. 5.

Sweetingham, Lisa. "Police rule Gotti girlfriend's death a suicide, but homicide case still open," CourtTV.com. Available online. URL: http://www.courttv.com. Posted on April 1, 2004.

Turkus, Burton B. and Sid Feder. *Murder Inc.: The Story of the Syndicate*. New York: Da Capo, 1992.

Tyler, Gus. *Organized Crime In America*. Ann Arbor: University of Michigan Press, 1962.

Weir, Richard, and Jane H. Furse. "Angel dares to tread: Sliwa honored, rips Gotti on mob don's old turf." *Daily News*, October 25, 2004, p. 19.

Whitehead, Don. *The FBI Story*. New York: Random House, 1956.

Zambito, Thomas. "Excedrin week looming for luckless Peter Gotti." *Daily News*, October 31, 2004, p. 34.

Further Resources

Books

Rolle, Andrew F. *The American Italians: Their History and Culture.* Belmont, Calif.: Wadsworth Publishing Company, 1972.

Simeone, John, and David Jacobs. *The Complete Idiot's Guide to the FBI.* New York: Alpha Books, 2003.

Torrance, Harold. *The JFK Assassination: Eye on History.* Redding, Calif.: Instructional Fair, 2002.

Web Sites

Crime Library
http://www.crimelibrary.com/

Federal Bureau of Investigation—Organized Crime
http://www.fbi.gov/hq/cid/orgcrime/ocshome.htm

"Organized Crime"
http://www.Infoplease.com

DVD

The World History of Organized Crime. New Video Group, Inc., 2001. *More than four hours long, traces the history of mob behavior globally and across time. Five episodes cover the mobs of China, India, Colombia, Russia, and Sicily.*

Index

Page numbers in *italics* indicate images.

About the Author

Michael Benson is the author or coauthor of 41 books, including the true-crime books *Betrayal in Blood* and *Lethal Embrace*. He's also written the *Encyclopedia of the JFK Assassination* and *Complete Idiot's Guides to NASA*, *National Security*, *The CIA*, *Submarines*, and *Modern China*. Other works include biographies of Ronald Reagan, Bill Clinton, and William Howard Taft. Originally from Rochester, N.Y., he is a graduate of Hofstra University.

About the Consulting Editor

John L. French is a 31-year veteran of the Baltimore City Police Crime Laboratory. He is currently a crime laboratory supervisor. His responsibilities include responding to crime scenes, overseeing the preservation and collection of evidence, and training crime scene technicians. He has been actively involved in writing the operating procedures and technical manual for his unit and has conducted training in numerous areas of crime scene investigation. In addition to his crime scene work, Mr. French is also a published author, specializing in crime fiction. His short stories have appeared in *Alfred Hitchcock's Mystery Magazine* and numerous anthologies.